D1617313

THE FUTURE AS NIGHTMARE

H. G. Wells and the Anti-utopians

MARK R. HILLEGAS

Southern Illinois University Press
CARBONDALE AND EDWARDSVILLE
Feffer & Simons, Inc.
LONDON AND AMSTERDAM

Library of Congress Cataloging in Publication Data

Hillegas, Mark Robert, 1926–
    The future as nightmare.

    (Arcturus books, AB123)
    Reprint of the ed. published by Oxford University
Press, New York.
    Bibliography: p.
    1. Wells, Herbert George, 1896–1946—Criticism and
interpretation.   2. Science fiction—History and
criticism.   3. Utopias in literature.   I. Title.
PR5777.H5   1974   823'.0876   74–4084
ISBN 0–8093–0680–8
ISBN 0–8093–0676–X (pbk.)

**ARCT
URUS
BOOKS** ®

Reprinted by arrangement with Mark R. Hillegas
Arcturus Books Edition September 1974
This edition printed by offset lithography
  in the United States of America

ACKNOWLEDGMENTS

I WISH TO record my thanks to the Research Council of Colgate University for grants for travel, photocopying, and the purchase of books, as well as for a fellowship which enabled me to begin to bring order to the material I had been gathering. For financial assistance as I completed the manuscript, I am grateful for the generosity of Southern Illinois University. To Professor Harris W. Wilson of the University of Illinois, I am indebted for a helpful introduction to the Wells Archive at Illinois.

For permission to quote from copyrighted material, I wish to thank various publishers, periodicals, and literary agents. In the United States I am indebted to the following: Brandt and Brandt for quotations from George Orwell's

Nineteen Eighty-four (copyright 1949 by Harcourt, Brace and World, Inc., reprinted by permission of Brandt and Brandt); E. P. Dutton, Inc., for quotations from Evgenii Zamyatin's *We*, trans. Gregory Zilboorg; Harcourt, Brace and World for quotations from George Orwell's *The Road to Wigan Pier* and *Dickens, Dali and Others* and for quotations from E. M. Forster's *Two Cheers for Democracy* and *The Eternal Moment and Other Stories*; Harper and Row, Publishers, for quotations from Aldous Huxley's *Brave New World* and *Point Counter Point* and for quotations from J. B. S. Haldane's *Possible Worlds*; The Macmillan Company for quotations from C. S. Lewis's *Out of the Silent Planet* and *That Hideous Strength*, for quotations from George Kateb's *Utopia and Its Enemies*, and for quotations from B. F. Skinner's *Walden Two*; *The Nation* for a quotation from Martin Green's "Distaste for the Contemporary"; Princeton University Press for quotations from Frederick C. Crews's *E. M. Forster: The Perils of Humanism*; Random House, Inc., for a quotation from Walter Van Tilburg Clark's "The Portable Phonograph," in *The Watchful Gods and Other Stories*; Scott Meredith Literary Agency, Inc., for a quotation from John Wyndham's *Re-Birth* (copyright 1955 by John Wyndham, reprinted by permission of the author and the author's agents, Scott Meredith Literary Agency, Inc.); Peter Smith, Publisher, for a quotation from Henry Adams's *The Degradation of the Democratic Dogma*; the University of Nebraska Press for quotations from H. G. Wells's *A Modern Utopia* (a Bison Book edition); W. W. Norton and Company, Inc., for quotations from Martin Green's *Science and the Shabby Curate of Poetry*; The Viking Press, Inc., for a quotation from Graham Greene's "A Discovery in the Woods," in *A Sense of Reality*; and Henry Z. Walck, Inc., for a quotation from Roger Lancelyn Green's *C. S. Lewis*.

In England I am indebted to the following: first of all,

to A. P. Watt and Son, Ltd., Literary Agents for the Estate of H. G. Wells, for numerous quotations from the writings of H. G. Wells; Arthur Barker, Ltd. for a quotation from Norman Nicholson's *H. G. Wells;* The Bodley Head, Ltd. for quotations from C. S. Lewis's *Out of the Silent Planet* and *That Hideous Strength;* A. M. Heath and Company, Ltd. for quotations from Karel Čapek's "The Meaning of R.U.R.," in the *Saturday Review* (London), July 21, 1923; and Longmans, Green and Co., Limited for quotations from Martin Green's *Science and the Shabby Curate of Poetry.*

Small portions of this book have appeared, in somewhat different form, in the *Papers of the Michigan Academy of Science, Arts, and Letters,* the *New Mexico Quarterly,* and in my Introduction to the University of Nebraska Press edition of H. G. Wells's *A Modern Utopia.* I wish to express my gratitude for permission to use this material here.

Finally, I wish to acknowledge a more general indebtedness to the encouragement or stimulus of certain individuals. My interest in the impact of science on the literary imagination began while studying at Columbia University some ten years ago, and accordingly I owe a debt to Professor Marjorie Hope Nicolson. Similarly, I must mention Professor Warner G. Rice of the University of Michigan: in discussions with him I came to see new dimensions to the problem of utopia and anti-utopia. I also value highly the many conversations about H. G. Wells which I have had with my friend Professor Richard H. Costa, now at Purdue University. And I am grateful for the valuable forum for the exchange of ideas which Professor Thomas D. Clareson of the College of Wooster has provided by keeping alive the MLA Conference on Science Fiction.

M. R. H.

Carbondale, Illinois
July 1967

ERRATUM

Page 17, line 34: *For* (1861) *read* (1961)

KEY TO ABBREVIATED CITATIONS

WELLS

TM	*The Time Machine*	in *Seven Science Fiction Novels of H. G. Wells.* New York, 1950.
IsM	*The Island of Dr. Moreau*	
WW	*The War of the Worlds*	
FMM	*The First Men in the Moon*	

| WSW | *When the Sleeper Wakes* | in *Three Prophetic Novels of H. G. Wells.* New York, 1952. |
| SDC | "A Story of the Days To Come" | |

MU   *A Modern Utopia.* Lincoln, Neb., 1967.

MLG *Men Like Gods,* in *28 Science Fiction Stories of H. G. Wells.* New York, 1952.

WA   *The War in the Air,* in *Three Science Fiction Novels by H. G. Wells.* New York, 1963.

FORSTER

MS   "The Machine Stops," in *The Eternal Moment*. London, 1928.

ČAPEK

R.U.R.   *R.U.R.*, in *Of Men and Machines*, ed. Arthur O. Lewis, Jr. New York, 1963.

ZAMYATIN

We   *We*, trans. Gregory Zilboorg. New York, 1959.
HW   *Herbert Wells*, in *Litsa* [Faces]. New York, 1955

HUXLEY

BNW   *Brave New World*. New York, 1946.

ORWELL

1984   *Nineteen Eighty-four*. New York, 1949.

LEWIS

OSP   *Out of the Silent Planet*. New York, 1944.
Perl   *Perelandra*. New York, 1944.
HS   *The Hideous Strength*. New York, 1946.

CONTENTS

THE FUTURE AS NIGHTMARE
H. G. Wells and the Anti-utopians

I<small>T IS A TRUISM</small> that one of the most revealing indexes to the anxieties of our age is the great flood of works like Zamyatin's *We,* Huxley's *Brave New World,* and Orwell's *Nineteen Eighty-four.* Appalling in their similarity, they describe nightmare states where men are conditioned to obedience, freedom is eliminated, and individuality crushed; where the past is systematically destroyed and men are isolated from nature; where science and technology are employed, not to enrich human life, but to maintain the state's surveillance and control of its slave citizens. Although sometimes given such names as *dystopias* or *cacotopias,* they have most often been called *anti-utopias* because they seem a sad, last farewell to man's age-old dream of a planned, ideal, and perfected society, a dream which appeared so noble in Plato's *Republic*, More's *Utopia*, Andreae's *Christianopolis*, and Bellamy's *Looking Backward*. In recent years, we are told, writers have seen the possibility of utopia approaching, but in the form of dictatorships, welfare states, planned economies, and all manner of bureaucracies, and they have become disillusioned. Thus the anti-utopias seem a phenomenon of our contemporary world, no older perhaps than the governments of Hitler, Stalin, or Roosevelt.

The explanation of the anti-utopian phenomenon in these familiar cultural and political terms is only partially correct, however, for it leaves out of consideration the fact that the modern anti-utopian tradition was shaped by an earlier and somewhat different world, that of the period from the 1890's to World War I. Overwhelmingly, the most important influences of this period in creating the modern anti-utopias were the scientific romances, utopias, and future histories of H. G. Wells, which, even when occasionally written after World War I, are still the unique product of this period.

There is nothing new, of course, in the idea that a relationship exists between H. G. Wells and the anti-utopias of the twentieth century. It can be found, for example, in G. Lowes Dickinson's praise in 1928 of Forster's "The Machine Stops" for turning the Shaw-Wells prophecies inside out, in George Orwell's praise in 1937 of Huxley's *Brave New World* for parodying Wells's vision of utopia, in Wyndham Lewis's description in 1952 of *Nineteen Eighty-four* as a Wellsian prophetic nightmare.[1] But none of those who have commented on this relationship have done more than note that certain anti-utopias are counter-Wellsian or that their general scheme is foreshadowed by Wells's complementary stories, *When the Sleeper Wakes* and "A Story of the Days To Come." Actually, it is a much more complex relationship, without whose exploration both H. G. Wells and

4

the twentieth-century anti-utopian phenomenon go only partially understood. In discussing it, I will follow three main lines of approach.

The first is that the great anti-utopias of the twentieth century constitute, with Wells's scientific romances, future histories, and, to some extent, utopias, a single kind of fiction, for which there is no other name than science fiction. Although Wells's work had various ancestors, it is from him that the writers of anti-utopias learned the uses of this form. Second, many of the central as well as peripheral images in the anti-utopias were first generated in Wells's early scientific romances, chiefly those written in the 1890's. Third, the relationship between Wells's writings and the major anti-utopias extends beyond images and form. To an extraordinary degree the great anti-utopias are both continuations of the imagination of H. G. Wells and reactions against that imagination. At the same time they often attack ideas that Wells championed, in many cases ideas which were in turn a protest against the decaying Victorian order of things. Altogether, it is doubtful that without Wells the anti-utopian phenomenon would ever have taken the shape it has.

Wells had this impact on anti-utopias because of his enormous popularity with the generation reaching maturity in the first decades of the twentieth century. All the major anti-utopians fall roughly into this generation: E. M. Forster was born in 1879, Evgenii Zamyatin in 1884, Aldous Huxley in 1894, C. S. Lewis in 1898, and George Orwell in 1903.

To many young people today, who have been taught that Wells lost the argument with Henry James about the "Novel," and escaped, as Mark Schorer put it, "from literature into the annals of an era," it may seem unlikely that Wells had any influence at all.[2] But an older generation would remember that from 1900 to 1920, and perhaps even to 1930, Wells was an angry young man fighting against

taboos and conventions, fighting against the whole of a plan-
less, greedy society. His impact was enormous, as dozens of
men, among them H. L. Mencken, Sinclair Lewis, André
Maurois, Eric Goldman, and Joseph Wood Krutch, have
testified. Thus Orwell wrote in 1945:

> Thinking people who were born about the beginning of this century
> are in some sense Wells's own creation. How much influence any
> mere writer has, and especially a "popular" writer whose work takes
> effect quickly, is questionable, but I doubt whether anyone who was
> writing books between 1900 and 1920, at any rate in the English lan-
> guage, influenced the young so much. The minds of all of us, and
> therefore the physical world, would be perceptibly different if Wells
> never existed.[3]

Wells was, said *The New York Times* in an editorial on the
occasion of his death in 1946, "the voice of the rising
generation of the Nineteen Hundreds" and the "greatest
public teacher of his time." [4] Or as J. I. M. Stewart has
recently written, "Upon youth—not literary youth merely,
but youth substantially and at large—no writer was to have a
comparable influence until George Orwell." [5]

But most intellectuals have long since rebelled against
Wells and the ideas he represented, so that F. R. Leavis
rather naturally used the phrase "crass Wellsianism" in
attacking C. P. Snow. Leavis rightly linked Snow with
Wells, but, as Martin Green remarked, whether one condemns Snow and Wells depends upon where one stands
with regard to two major but antithetical movements in the
intellectual life of England in the twentieth century. The
spirit of the first, said Green, "was summed up in Wells's
three huge compilations, *An Outline of History, The Science of Life,* and *The Work, Wealth, and Happiness of
Mankind;* a spirit of broad general knowledge, national and
international planning, optimism about (or at least cheerful
businesslike engagement with) the powers of contemporary

6

science and technology, and a philistinism about the more esoteric manifestations of art and religion." The second movement, which began its ascendancy in the 1920's, insists on narrow intense knowledge (insights), on the need for personal freedom within the best-planned society, on the dangers of modern science and technology, on the irreducibility of artistic and religious modes." [6] The paradigm of the confrontation between these two movements, as Green aptly pointed out, is the quarrel between Henry James and H. G. Wells. But anyone who has read the full record of that quarrel in Gordon Ray and Leon Edel's *Henry James and H. G. Wells* would have to agree that wisdom and humanity are hardly the exclusive possession of either side.

II

Since the great anti-utopias, along with many of Wells's writings, are what we have called "science fiction," we need to define it and explain the relationship of Wells's work to other examples of the form. Admittedly in talking about this subject one runs the risk of not being taken seriously, in large part because of the connotations of the term itself. Coined in 1929 by the pulp publisher Hugo Gernsback, it has come for many educated people to mean the supposed worst excesses of the pulp magazines: creaking plots and cheap sensationalism, characters of cardboard and glue, a prose style to set one's teeth on edge, perhaps a degrading obsession with gadgets and machines. And so most people have dismissed science fiction as fit at best for what T. S. Eliot once called the "pre-adolescent imagination," though a few others, like J. O. Bailey in *Pilgrims Through Space and Time*, Sam Moskowitz in *Seekers of Tomorrow*, and Kingsley Amis in *New Maps of Hell*, have found much to praise. Often, though by no means always, science fiction's bad reputation has been deserved, particularly so in the early novels and stories in the magazines. But deserved or not, this reputation has had one very unfortunate consequence: it has prevented recognition of the fact that there exist novels and stories similar to pulp science fiction in their conventions and themes but greatly superior in their literary quality and significance of comment on human life. It is this superior science fiction with which this book is concerned and which at the moment we are trying to define.

Here Amis's definition makes a very good beginning. "Science fiction," he wrote, "is that class of prose narrative treating of a situation that could not arise in the world we know, but which is hypothesised on the basis of some innovation in science or technology, or pseudo-science or pseudo-technology." [7] It is distinguished from pure fantasy by its need to achieve verisimilitude and win the "willing suspension of disbelief" through scientific plausibility. To this definition Amis adds two codicils, kinds of narratives which he includes because they appeal to the same set of interests or are written and read by the same writers and readers. The first category—stories about prehistoric man—is important for our discussion because it includes William Golding's *The Inheritors*. The second category, of little interest to us, consists of stories "based on some change or disturbance or local anomaly in physical conditions," very often the threatened destruction of earthly life in a worldwide or cosmic disaster.

To Amis's definition we must make certain additions. The first is the extremely important one—that "quality" science fiction, such as is represented by the great anti-utopias, always makes a significant comment on human life: usually it is a vehicle for social criticism and satire. Then we must discriminate between science fiction and satiric utopia. While science fiction can be satiric and borrows techniques from the satiric utopia, as it does in the case of *Brave New World,* the pure satiric utopia, such as *Erewhon,* is not science fiction. In the satiric utopia, the author assumes a more ironic attitude toward his subject and is not as consistently serious about achieving verisimilitude, whether scientific or otherwise. Or put another way, the writer of science fiction presents what he intends to be taken as actual possibilities, whereas the satiric utopist can be more tongue in cheek about what he presents, at least once he gets his reader to his imaginary world. What the satiric utopist usually offers in this other world are inversions, parodies, or grotesque variations of things in our world—thus Butler's Musical Banks or his College of Unreason, thus Swift's Lilliputian courtiers who dance under ribbons or walk tightropes to win preferment. In science fiction, on the other hand, the fundamental principle is prediction or extrapolation, from existing knowledge and conditions, of things to come. But, of course, mixture of the two forms can occur; and occasionally science fiction (such as some of the work of Frederik Pohl) seems to be almost pure satiric utopia.

As we have defined science fiction (chiefly following Amis), it is pre-eminently a modern phenomenon, but works which more or less fit our formula exist at least as early as the seventeenth century, so that the whole tradition needs to be related to our discussion. This kind of literature had its beginning under the stimulus of the first scientific revolution: Bacon's *New Atlantis* (1624), with its House of Salomon and its various prophecies of scientific marvels, such as submarines and aircraft, is surely in part science fiction. More important than the *New Atlantis* in the seventeenth century as science fiction are the cosmic voyages, which Marjorie Nicolson discussed in her *Voyages to the Moon* and which she showed to be the response of the literary imagination to the new astronomy—works like Kepler's *Somnium*

(1634), Godwin's *The Man in the Moone* (1638), and Cyrano de Bergerac's *Voyages to the Sun and Moon* (1650). In the eighteenth century, cosmic voyages continued to be written, though most are trivial, and in this connection one should note that probably only the "Voyage to Laputa" in *Gulliver's Travels* is significant as science fiction (as Professor Nicolson shows, it is actually a moon voyage in reverse).

But in the nineteenth century, a period of astonishingly fertile scientific activity and of technological developments which completely changed the conditions of human life, science fiction really began to flourish. Under the impact of Herschel's new descriptive astronomy, and the discoveries about the limits of the atmosphere that resulted from the invention of the balloon, cosmic voyages proliferated and became much more realistic. Meanwhile there also appeared many other varieties of science fiction, represented by such varied works as Hawthorne's "The Birthmark," Poe's "The Facts in the Case of M. Valdemar," Mary Shelley's *Frankenstein,* and Robert Louis Stevenson's "Dr. Jekyll and Mr. Hyde." Some utopias, particularly late in the century, contained science-fiction elements: thus Bellamy's *Looking Backward* and Hertzka's *Freeland,* but especially the German "technological utopias," such as Lasswitz' *Auf Zwei Planeten* (also a variety of the cosmic voyage, the "Martian romance"). But by far the most important development of science fiction appeared in the writings of Jules Verne. In a sense, Verne prepared the way for Wells, whose science fiction in turn molded the anti-utopias of the twentieth century.

The sheer volume of Verne's output—usually one or two books a year from 1863 to 1905—and his extraordinary popularity explain his influence. Not all of his "Voyages extraordinaires," of course, are science fiction, for many are tales of adventure, appealing to the romantic interests of the nineteenth century—stories of journeys on rafts up the Amazon, of castaways marooned like Crusoe on desert islands, of expeditions to the pole, of journeys around the world in eighty days or into the heart of unexplored Africa. Nor was Verne a great writer in terms of characterization or sophistication of style, but at times he rose to a poetry, if not of expression, at least of imaginative conception. As far as his science fiction is concerned, he did this most notably at the beginning of his career, in *A Journey to the Center of the Earth* (1864), *From the Earth to the Moon* (1865) and *Around the Moon* (1870), and *Twenty Thousand Leagues Under the Sea* (1870). In these books he was, as Kenneth Allott has shown, the almost archetypal expression of nineteenth-century romantic interest in science and technology.[8] In this respect his greatest contribution was to establish in the public consciousness science fiction as a distinct mode of writing. Although he had only slight direct influence on Wells, his writings helped to create the readership for the much more important scientific romances and stories which Wells began writing in the 1890's.

Wells's early scientific romances, which launched his career as writer and prophet, not only sold well and were read widely, but they reached a much more sophisticated audience than the books which Verne created. Verne never received the kind of attention from serious writers that was given to Wells. Thus the master, Henry James, filled with "wonder and admiration" for Wells's early stories and scientific romances, spoke of reading *The First Men in the Moon* "*à petites doses* as one sips (I suppose) old Tokay," and of allowing *Twelve Stories and a Dream* "to melt lollipopwise, upon my imaginative tongue."[9] Joseph Conrad wrote to Wells how much he liked his work, particularly *The Invisible Man:* "Impressed is *the* word, O Realist of the Fantastic!" Of *The Invisible Man*, he added, "It is masterly—it is ironic—it is very relentless—and it is very true." [10] In the 1890's and in the first years of the twentieth century, other writers—Bennett, Shaw, Gissing, Galsworthy—similarly admired the gifts of storytelling and the vitality of imagination displayed in Wells's early stories and scientific romances. The reviewers—when they chose to notice—were generally favorably disposed. W. T. Stead, editor of the powerful *Review of Reviews*, welcomed *The Time Machine*—Wells's first major publication—as the work of a man of genius, and the *Spectator*, reviewing *The War of the Worlds*, concluded that Wells, at least in the writing of scientific romances, was Poe's superior. [11]

And so it is that because of the power and immediacy of his ideas, because of the quality and sophistication of his imagination, because of his skill as a writer, Wells's scientific romances and stories have exerted a powerful influence on the development of science fiction in our century. In passing I should also note, although it is not the subject of this book, that Wells had great impact on the lower reaches of science fiction, beginning with the first issues of Hugo Gernsback's *Amazing* in 1926. For years pulp writers, at first interested in adventure and sensational effects, took ideas from Wells, who had developed or invented such themes as time travel, the destruction of earth by cosmic accident, the return of mankind to barbarism after the collapse of civilization, the journey to another world in space, the invasion from space, all to comment on life in a mechanical and scientific age. (His influence was also felt indirectly through the writings of Olaf Stapledon, whose *Last and First Men* (1930) and *The Star Maker* (1937), both heavily indebted to Wells, became a mine of ideas for pulp stories.) But for us his most important impact is not only on such works as *We, Brave New World*, and *Nineteen Eighty-four*, but also on others, like Forster's "The Machine Stops" and C. S. Lewis's "cosmic trilogy," as well as occasional works of quality by professional science-fiction writers, such as Ray Bradbury's *Fahrenheit 451*, Kurt Vonnegut, Jr.'s *Player Piano*, and Walter Miller, Jr.'s *A Canticle for Leibowitz*.

III

Wells turned naturally and easily to the writing of science fiction because he possessed what demands to be called "the Wellsian imagination." This Wellsian imagination is the key to his science fiction as well as to the nature of its impact, and I shall attempt to describe it briefly.

Wells is, of course, closely identified with a particular vision of a utopian World State, a vision which is important in explaining his relationship to the anti-utopians and which I will discuss at length in a subsequent chapter devoted largely to his utopias. What I am dealing with now, however, is a quality, a way of looking at things, which was first described at length by Van Wyck Brooks in 1915.[12] This quality, which must surely be a chief characteristic of the mind scientifically educated, is detachment. As Brooks remarked about Wells's fiction in general, and as we would say particularly about his scientific romances, future histories, and utopias, Wells saw men chemically and anatomically, the world astronomically. Brooks also put it another way: it is the distinction between the intellectual, who views life in terms of ideas, and the artist, who views life in terms of experience. Generally speaking, the intellectual dominated Wells's writings, though sometimes—most continuously in *Tono-Bungay*, *Kipps*, and *Mr. Polly*—the artist took over. But it must be emphasized that this distinction between "intellectual" and "artistic" refers to the angle at which reality is viewed, not to the quality of writing. Even at his most "intellectual," as in, say, *The Time Machine*, Wells was capable of vividness in both conception and expression. *The Time Machine*, though it differs greatly from ordinary fiction, has some right to the title of "art."

Surely the single most spectacular manifestation of this detached quality of the Wellsian imagination is its preoccupation with the future. This preoccupation, which is central to many of Wells's writings, is most enthusiastically explained in "The Discovery of the Future," a lecture Wells delivered at the Royal Institution in January 1902, which was published in *Nature* the next month. In this lecture, Wells distinguished between two kinds of minds. The first, oriented to the past, regards the future "as sort of black nonexistence upon which the advancing present will presently write events." It is the legal mind, always referring to precedents. The second kind of mind, oriented to the future, is constructive, creative, organizing. "It sees the world as one great workshop, and the present is no more than material for the future, for the thing that is yet destined to be." [13] Finally, Wells predicted what might be accomplished if the future-oriented mind were given freedom to express itself:

All this world is heavy with the promise of greater things, and a day will come, one day in the unending succession of days, when beings who are now latent in our thoughts and hidden in our loins, shall stand upon this earth as one stands upon a footstool and shall laugh and reach out their hands amidst the stars." [14]

(In the context of that entire lecture, this passage is not, incidentally, the expression of simple optimism it can easily be taken to be.)

Along with the detached imagination and its preoccupation with the future go certain clearly defined and inevitable values and interests. Wells—not surprisingly for a former student and admirer of T. H. Huxley—was a supreme rationalist and believer in science and the scientific method, a

Francis Bacon reborn. And so for Wells, as for one of his Utopians in *Men Like Gods*, there was no way out of the cages of life but by knowledge—knowledge of man himself and of man in relation to the things about him. Naturally the Wellsian imagination is drawn to certain characteristic subjects. It is fascinated by the revelations of man's place in time and space given to us by science, fascinated by the vistas of astronomy, particularly the death of the world and the vastness of interstellar space, fascinated by the vision of geological epochs, the evolution of life, and the early history of man vouchsafed by geology, paleontology, and archaeology.

The first, brilliant fruit of this Wellsian imagination were the scientific romances and stories written in the 1890's which led, in their turn, by a complicated process which also involved reaction against the Wellsian utopias, to the major anti-utopias of the twentieth century.

IRONICALLY, Wells's early scientific romances and stories present a vision of man's nature, his place in the universe, and the power of science which is the complete antithesis of the vision that by the 1930's was commonly considered Wellsian. "Wellsian," it need hardly be said, came to connote a utopia filled with super-gadgets, mechanical wonders, run by an elite of scientists and engineers for the good of the people (the kind of thing the public saw in the tasteless movie made by Alexander Korda, *Things to Come*). The application of science had almost automatically brought this heaven on earth, which was inhabited by a finer race of human beings, who had inevitably evolved to their state of near perfection. Neither in spirit nor in detail are Wells's stories and romances at all similar to this commonly accepted notion of the Wellsian vision.

Odd as it may seem in view of the later widespread identification of Wells with scientific optimism, knowledgeable commentators have long been aware of the darkness which actually permeates much of the early science fiction—the stories and the great scientific romances like *The Time Machine, The Invisible Man, The Island of Dr. Moreau, The War of the Worlds,* and *The First Men in the Moon.* In the 1890's several reviewers, one of whom was W. T. Stead, were quick to note Wells's pessimism and "the gloomy horror of his vision." [1] Certain later critics have been well aware that the Wells of the scientific romances is not "Wellsian." Thus Geoffrey West in 1930 saw Wells "querying mankind's complacent sovereignty of the future"; [2] thus Norman Nicholson wrote in 1950:

Wells was aware from the first that the development of scientific knowledge was not in itself any guarantee of progress, and many of his romances are based on the idea that science divorced from humanity and from the wisdom that sees beyond the first line of consequence, may bring disaster to mankind. Several of his romances are warnings of what may happen if technological development gets out of hand, and others deal with the destruction of civilization by cosmic catastrophe. It is surely significant that the man who preached progress more eloquently than anyone else should be the one who had the most vivid vision of cosmic accident, and who realized that civilization is as frail a thing as human life, and that the destiny of the whole earth, no less than that of its inhabitants, hangs by a thread.[3]

More recently, in 1957, Anthony West in a challenging article in *Encounter* supported the thesis, chiefly by reference to the scientific romances, that Wells was "by nature a pessimist." [4] Likewise, Bernard Bergonzi in *The Early H. G. Wells* (1861) demonstrated at length the pessimism in the stories and the scientific romances, even going to the extreme of relating them to nineteenth-century *fin de siècle*.[5]

To understand the darkness and pessimism of the early stories and scientific romances, we must remember that they were written against the background of grave social injustice and economic distress, socialist agitation and labor unrest.[6] Fifty years after Disraeli had written of the "two nations," England still consisted chiefly of the rich and the poor. At the bottom of the social heap were the exploited multitudes of the industrial proletariat, who, in spite of the fact that conditions had improved incredibly since the "Hungry Forties," still led horribly deformed and meaningless lives. Above them were the energetic and upward aspiring middle class, cramped by the conditions of their existence only at the bottom levels of the class. At the summit, the "unpremeditated, successful, aimless Plutocracy" led sterile lives of unproductive leisure. The middle and upper classes, who were seldom their brothers' keepers and usually ignored the inhabitants of the Abyss, managed, in the face of worsening conditions during these last years of the nineteenth century, to hold to their faith in "progress," managed to believe that things were somehow improving. In his scientific romances and stories written at this time, Wells set about vigorously to attack this late Victorian complacency, for in his opinion there was no greater enemy of progress than a belief in inevitable progress. He launched this attack, as I have pointed out elsewhere,[7] from what is best described as the "cosmic pessimism" of T. H. Huxley.

When in the 1880's the shabby and underfed young Wells was a scholarship student at the Normal School of Science, beginning what he had at first hoped would be a great scientific career, there was no greater man in his estimation than Thomas Henry Huxley. Of Huxley's impact, Wells wrote in 1901:

I do not know if the students of to-day will quite understand how we felt for our Dean—we read his speeches, we borrowed the books he wrote, we clubbed out of our weekly guineas to buy the *Nineteenth Century* whenever he rattled Gladstone or pounded the Duke of Argyle. I believed then that he was the greatest man I was likely to meet, and I believe that all the more firmly to-day.[8]

In 1904 Wells described the kind of education he received at South Kensington—"three years of illuminating and good scientific work" which gave him "an exceptionally clear and ordered view of the ostensibly real universe." "I had man definitely placed in the great scheme of space and time."[9] Most important for the scientific romances, Huxley shaped Wells's philosophy of nature and evolution: "Of all the philosophical interpretations of Darwin," W. Warren Wagar wrote, "[Wells] had no use for any but T. H. Huxley's."[10] This interpretation is most extensively stated in Huxley's famous Romanes lecture, *Evolution and Ethics* (1894), though it is also present in other writings of Huxley's. There can be little question of Wells's indebtedness to Huxley for a philosophy of evolution, for not only is there the evidence of the scientific romances themselves but there is also Wells's essay, "Human Evolution, An Artificial Process," in the October 1, 1896, *Fortnightly Review,* which is obviously derivative from Huxley, particularly the Romanes lecture.

In Huxley's philosophy of evolution there is an element of grave doubt about the outcome of the cosmic or evolutionary process—his "cosmic pessimism"—which was exactly suited to Wells's aesthetic and didactic purposes in the stories and scientific romances written in the 1890's. And it is this "cosmic pessimism" which inspired the details in the scientific romances (chiefly *The Time Machine, The Island of Dr. Moreau, When the Sleeper Wakes* and "A Story of the Days To Come," and *The First Men in the Moon*) that are repeated in the works by Forster, Zamyatin, Huxley, Orwell, and others and that make these romances by Wells something like the first modern anti-utopias.

By the 1880's Huxley had clearly formulated his idea that the evolutionary process will never lead to moral or social improvement, for cosmic nature is the "headquarters of the enemy of ethical nature" and the only chance for social and ethical progress is the "checking of the cosmic process at every step" and the substitution for it of the ethical.[11] But, as Houston Peterson remarked, Huxley had "no fantastic hopes" for the success of any such effort.[12] The savagery in civilized men will not easily be eradicated because their cosmic nature is the outcome of millions of years of evolutionary training, while control of the cosmic process by manipulating the human organism is out of the question. Occasionally Huxley became so pessimistic that he would almost have welcomed "some kindly comet" to sweep the whole affair away.

Not only did the theory of evolution for Huxley encourage "no millennial anticipations" as to man's hope for a better life on earth, but it also indicated that eventually the cosmic process will destroy man. Evolution involves a "constant remodeling of the organism in adaptation to new conditions," but it depends upon the nature of these conditions whether the modifications will be upward or downward. Retrogressive change is just as possible and practicable as progressive. If, as Huxley considered most likely, the belief of the physicists is true that the Earth is gradually cooling down, "then the time will come when evolution will mean an adaptation to a universal winter, and all forms of life will die out, except such low and simple organisms as the Diatom of the arctic and antarctic ice and the Protococcus of red snow." For Huxley the course of life upon the surface of the earth was like the trajectory of "a ball fired from a mortar," and "the sinking half of that course is as much a part of the general process of evolution as the rising." And Huxley doubted that, when the decline begins, man will be able to stop it. "If, for millions of years, our globe has taken the upward road," he wrote, "yet, some time the summit will be reached and the downward route will be commenced. The most daring imagination will hardly venture upon the suggestion that the power and intelligence of man can ever arrest the procession of the great year." [13]

II

The detached Wellsian imagination, obsessed by the Huxleyan cosmic pessimism, led Wells in the 1890's to produce two categories of attack on human complacency. The first and larger group contains stories chiefly of pure menace, and excellent fiction they are indeed, being among the very best things of this sort ever written. The second category, closely related to the first, consists of works anti-utopian in their assault on optimism.

The germ of the stories of menace, and probably of the one romance of the same type, is contained in an article Wells published in the *Pall Mall Gazette*, September 25, 1894, and entitled "The Extinction of Man," an article which relates these stories and the romance to Wells's interest in the future. Wells began "The Extinction of Man" by questioning man's complacent assumption of his continued existence on this planet in the light of the evidence from geology: "in no case does the record of the fossils show a really dominant species succeeded by its own descendants." It is the familiar lesson of geology; again and again forms of life have risen to dominance, only to vanish away and be replaced by other forms:

What has usually happened in the past appears to be the emergence of some type of animal hitherto rare and unimportant, and the extinction, not simply of the previously ruling species, but of most of the forms that are at all closely related to it. Sometimes, indeed, as in the case of the extinct giants of South America, they vanished without any considerable rivals, victims of pestilence, famine, or, it may be, of that cumulative inefficiency that comes of a too undisputed life.[14]

And so Wells came to caution his readers against the "too acceptable view of man's certain tenure of the earth for the next few million years or so." As possible threats, he cited, among others, the evolution of the ant and the cephalopod, thus foreshadowing two of his stories, "The Empire of the Ants" and "The Sea Raiders."

Wells ended his article with a repetition of his warning in a passage which makes clear his intention to attack complacency:

No; man's complacent assumption of the future is too confident. We think, because things have been easy for mankind as a whole for a generation or so, we are going on to perfect comfort and security in the future. We think that we shall always go to work at ten and leave off at four and have dinner at seven forever and ever. But these four suggestions out of a host of others must surely do a little against this complacency. Even now, for all we can tell, the coming terror may be crouching for its spring and the fall of humanity be at hand. In the case of every other predominant animal the world has ever seen, I repeat, the hour of its complete ascendency has been the eve of its entire overthrow.[15]

And so Wells wrote numerous stories of menace. "The Empire of the Ants" (1905) describes a race of intelligent ants in the upper region of the Amazon who are beginning a march on civilization—"new competitors for the sovereignty of the globe." "The Sea Raiders" (1896) purports to be a "true account" of the attack on the coast of Devon and Cornwall of giant man-eating octupuses. "The Flowering of the Strange Orchid" (1894) deals with a man-eating plant; "In the Avu Observatory" (1894) with a giant and hostile bat; "The Valley of the Spiders" (1903) with a deadly floating spider. But the best of the stories is "The Star" (1897), which deals, in remarkably solid, concrete detail, with the catastrophic approach to the earth of a large body of matter from the depths of space beyond the solar system.

Disaster also comes from outer space in the one scientific romance of pure menace type that Wells wrote and which is closely related to "The Star" and "The Sea Raiders"—the enormously effective *The War of the Worlds* (1898). In plot and fictional technique it bears some resemblance to Defoe's *A Journal of the Plague Year:* both novels are offered as eyewitness accounts of a great disaster which befalls mankind and particularly the inhabitants of London. In each case the disaster had a special topical interest at the time of publication: an outbreak of the plague in 1720 in Marseilles set Londoners to recalling the horror of 1665, while in the 1890's popular interest in Mars as the abode of life was, because of Schiaparelli's earlier discovery of the "canals," so intense that it at times amounted to a mania.[16] At the same time this interest combines with a fascination for stories of an invasion of England which began, as I. F. Clarke has shown in *Voices Prophesying War,* with Sir George Chesney's "Battle of Dorking" (1872).[17]

In *The War of the Worlds,* the Martians, "minds that are to our minds as ours are to those of the beasts that perish, intellects vast and cool and unsympathetic," look longingly at our young green world and decide to take it from us. The inevitable process of planetary cooling, which was predicted in the nineteenth century from the Second Law of Thermodynamics, has already proceeded far on Mars, and the invaders are driven from their planet, as one day we too will be forced into space to find a new home. "The last stage of exhaustion, which to us is still incredibly remote, has become a present-day problem for the inhabitants of Mars" (p. 310). Hurtling through space come the Martians to put us to rout with their superior machines, their heat ray, their poisonous gas, only to die suddenly and unexpectedly from terrestrial diseases to which they have long since lost immunity. The war between the planets is thus prophetic of the holocaust of World War I and its airplanes, submarines, tanks, and poisonous gas: a warning of the changes in human life to be brought by new science and technology.

The controlling principle in the narration of these events is the contrast between the invasion and the calm, secure, snug Victorian world to which it comes, and in this narration Wells achieved magnificent verisimilitude by the use of circumstantial detail. The climax comes when the Martians march relentlessly on London. As a roaring wave of fear sweeps through the greatest city in the world, its social organization collapses. London's populace pours out of the city—"a stampede gigantic and terrible—without order and without goal, six million people, unarmed and unprovisioned, driven headlong" (p. 390). It is the end of civilization.

Obviously *The War of the Worlds* is intended to attack human complacency, as the narrator himself reminds us in discussing the benefits which, "in the larger design of the universe," have come from the invasion. "It has robbed us," he notes, " of that serene self-confidence in the future which is the most fruitful source of decadence" (p. 452).

III

Much more important for our purposes than the story of menace is the second category of Wellsian attack on human complacency, in which Huxleyan cosmic pessimism generates images and ideas central to the twentieth-century anti-utopian tradition. The major works in this "cosmic pessimism" category are *The Time Machine, The Island of Dr. Moreau, When the Sleeper Wakes,* "A Story of the Days To Come," and *The First Men in the Moon.* There are, of course, a few other stories or romances which may be manifestations of the Huxleyan cosmic pessimism, but they are not influential enough in the anti-utopian tradition to be discussed at any length. One of these is *The Invisible Man,* which we will study briefly as it relates to *The Island of Dr. Moreau.* Another is *The Food of the Gods,* a fable so seriously flawed by an unwarranted shift from a brilliantly comic beginning to a serious and prophetic end that its influence is slight and we can ignore it entirely. Still another romance, "A Story of the Stone Age," we will look at briefly in the section of the Epilogue devoted to William Golding's attack on utopia. As for "In the Days of the Comet," one of Wells's less successful scientific romances, it is best described as a scientific romance passing into a utopia, and with this comment dismissed.

Our discussion properly begins with *The Time Machine* (1895), the first of Wells's scientific romances and perhaps the most nearly faultless example of the kind of fiction with which we are concerned. Its vitality and literary power are enormous, its credibility almost perfect, and, inspired by Huxleyan cosmic pessimism, it is rich in significant meanings. It is worth discussing its technique, not only to show how this kind of fiction works, but also to explain why *The Time Machine* had such an enormous impact on the twentieth-century anti-utopia.

"For the writer of fantastic stories to help the reader to play the game properly," Wells wrote, "he must help him in every possible unobtrusive way to *domesticate* the impossible hypothesis. He must trick him into an unwary concession to some plausible assumption and get on with his story while the illusion holds." [18] This is exactly Wells's technique in *The Time Machine*.

And so the story begins in the solid, upper-middle-class atmosphere of the Time Traveler's home, as he is expounding to his guests after dinner the mysteries of the geometry of Four Dimensions:

"I do not mean to ask you to accept anything without reasonable ground for it. You will soon admit as much as I need from you. You know of course that a mathematical line, a line of thickness *nil*, has no real existence. They taught you that? Neither has a mathematical plane. These things are mere abstractions."

"That is all right," said the Psychologist.

"Nor, having only length, breadth, and thickness, can a cube have a real existence."

"There I object," said Filby. "Of course a solid body may exist. All real things——"

"So most people think. But wait a moment. Can an *instantaneous* cube exist?" (*TM* 3)

Before we know what has happened, we are tricked into the concession that Time could be another, a Fourth Dimension, along which one might travel as one does the other three dimensions. All we need is a vehicle.

And so Wells invented the Time Machine, thereby becoming the father of a new genre, the modern story of time travel. The invention was a major leap of the imagination, and it grew not only out of contemporary interest in the geometry of four dimensions but also the great vogue at the time for tales of the future. Such stories existed, of course, at least as early as Mercier's *L'An 2440* (1772), but their wide popularity began only with Edward Bellamy's *Looking Backward* (1888). In the late 1880's and early 1890's, dozens of these stories were written, and at least two besides *Looking Backward* are significant as literature: W. H. Hudson's *A Crystal Age* (1888) and William Morris's *News from No-*

where (1891). *The Time Machine* is a natural evolution from all these stories and an improvement on them, for in each the visitor arrives in the future by means of such clumsy devices as dream, hypnosis, accident, or trance. Wells's machine is considerably more suitable, given the sophisticated requirements for plausibility of a new scientific and mechanical age. It may possibly have been suggested to him by the space vehicle of the cosmic voyage, obviously a related genre.[19]

In any case, the Time Traveler, allowing his guests no opportunity to think of objections to his theory of Time as the Fourth Dimension, fetches a working model of his invention. It vanishes into the future, and then he takes his guests, whose skepticism is seriously shaken, to see the Time Machine itself. As always in the best of his scientific romances and stories, Wells's use of circumstantial detail is magnificent: the long, draughty corridor to the laboratory, the flickering candlelight, the silhouette of the Time Traveler's broad head. Finally, the description of the machine—solid, specific in details, vague as to over-all design:

Parts were of nickel, parts of ivory, parts had certainly been filed or sawn out of rock crystal. The thing was generally complete, but the twisted crystalline bars lay unfinished upon the bench beside some sheets of drawings, and I took one up for a better look at it. Quartz it seemed to be. (*TM* 10)

So ends the first Thursday evening. A week later the guests are again assembled for dinner, when the Time Traveler returns from the future, dirty, dusty, disheveled, and limping on tattered blood-stained socks. And so the tale proper begins as the Time Traveler recounts his adventures.

It is impossible, really, to do justice to the perfection of Wells's effort to ease the reader into a willing suspension of disbelief in these first two framing chapters. All one can do is list some of the elements: the common-sense character of

the narrator; the solid atmosphere of his home; the characterization of the guests to give them sufficient—but not too
much—individuality for the purposes of the story; the skill-
ful use of incidental details to create the air of reality. This
same perfection continues in the next section, the journey
through time to the year 802,701, and, indeed, throughout
the rest of the romance.

In the description of the journey through time, Wells's
powers of concretization, apparent throughout the story, are
at their highest. The journey begins, as do most journeys
into space in fiction and reality, with a shock at departure:
"I drew a breath, set my teeth, gripped the starting lever
with both hands, and went off with a thud" (p. 15). The
sensations of time travel are those of motion through space,
and at first the Time Traveler finds them distinctly unpleasant. He has a feeling of helpless headlong motion and
the horrible anticipation of an imminent collision. Later, the
unpleasant nature of time travel begins to wear off and the
Traveler experiences the kind of exhilaration felt by many
voyagers through space in fiction from Domingo Gonsales
and Cyrano de Bergerac to Elwin Ransom. Finally he
watches awestruck the accelerated sequence of celestial phe-
nomena. He sees the moon spinning swiftly through her
quarters from new to full, the alternation of day and night
merging into one continuous grayness, the sky taking on a
wonderful deepness of blue, and the sun, like a streak of fire,
burning a brilliant arch in space. As his velocity increases at a
tremendous rate, he becomes apprehensive and decides to
stop, and in his panic slows the machine down too suddenly.
Traveler and machine go toppling over into the world of
802,701. Thunder rumbles and hail hisses around him as he
sits on the grass of what seems to be a little garden.

This world, as we will see later, is central to the meaning
of *The Time Machine*. Suffice it now to say that it is a dis-

illusionment to the Traveler. Instead of a world far advanced beyond ours, he finds that in 802,701 mankind has evolved into two degenerate species: above ground, the Eloi, delicate little creatures with the intellect of a five-year-old; and below ground, the pale, ape-like Morlocks, who leave their subterranean world only at night. It is the sunset of mankind.

But at first glance, the earth in 802,701 seems to be a garden of Eden. Everywhere are beautiful flowers and fruit, and no hostile insects or animals—nature is seemingly in perfect subjugation to man. The weather is mild and warm, apparently because the earth is now closer to a sun into which have fallen one or more of the inner planets. Gone are the smaller houses and cottages of our time; instead our descendants live in magnificent, ornate palace-like buildings "dotted about among the variegated greenery." These are the buildings of utopia and the first manifestation of Wells's familiar preoccupation with housing and the physical features of the future.

But a second look reveals that it is only a ruined splendor. All human artifacts are slowly crumbling. Some of the buildings are already gone: "a great heap of granite, bound together by masses of aluminium, a vast labyrinth of precipitous walls and crumbled heaps, amidst which were thick heaps of very beautiful pagoda-like plants." And even the many still-standing buildings, in which the surface people live, are decaying:

And perhaps the thing that struck me most was its dilapidated look. The stained-glass windows, which displayed only a geometrical pattern, were broken in many places, and the curtains that hung across the lower end were thick with dust. And it caught my eye that the corner of the marble table near me was fractured. (TM 22)

Even more of a ruined splendor are the people the Time Traveler finds living in this great garden—the Eloi. Fragile little creatures perhaps four feet tall, they pass their time "in playing gently, in bathing in the river, in making love in a half-playful fashion, in eating fruit and sleeping." Human vigor and energy have passed into languor and decay.

In time the Traveler learns the purpose of the mysterious wells and towers scattered across the country: these structures are part of the ventilation system for a subterranean world, in which live the other degenerate descendants of men, the Morlocks. They are strange little beings whose pallid bodies are "just the half-bleached colour of the worms and things one sees preserved in spirit in a zoological museum." They are chinless, and in their faces are set "great lidless, pinkish grey eyes." At night they leave their subterranean world to hunt down Eloi for food.

Slowly the Time Traveler pieces together the history of mankind's horrible degeneration, a degeneration which has occurred because mankind, as T. H. Huxley feared, was ultimately unable to control the cosmic or evolutionary process. It is Huxley's cosmic pessimism which gives meaning and permanence to this first anti-utopia of the modern mechanical and scientific age. For all its exuberance and vitality of imagination, *The Time Machine* is a bleak and sober vision of man's place in the universe. By the year 800,000, the world, at least above ground, had become intelligent and co-operative, truly a modern utopia. Nature had been subjugated and man had readjusted the balance of animal and vegetable life to suit his needs. Disease, hardship, and poverty were eliminated. With the attainment of security and freedom from danger, man's restless energy turned to art, and for a time a great culture flourished. But it was a utopian age which could never last because the upper-worlders ignored another of Huxley's warnings: "If we may permit ourselves a larger hope of abatement of the essential evil of the world . . . I deem it an essential condition of the realization of that hope that we cast aside the notion that escape from pain and sorrow is the proper object of life." [20] And so came languor and decay. The struggle to conquer nature had developed human intelligence, strength, and courage. But when the battle had been won, there was no force to select the most fit. In the new state of balance and security, intellectual and physical power were out of place. The weak were as well equipped as the strong, in fact even better equipped, for the strong were fretted by an energy for which there was no outlet. And so the inhabitants of the utopia above ground evolved to feeble prettiness, a process which constitutes one of the major criticisms in the twentieth century of the idea of utopia. The perfection and ease of utopia, say many of its critics—like Forster in "The Machine Stops"—can only lead to degeneration and decay.

But this was only half the explanation of the world of 802,701. The development of the Morlocks had followed a somewhat different course, and here the story becomes social criticism and very much a product of the 1890's, the years of increasing Socialist protest. The Eloi and Morlocks grew apart, just as earlier in the nineteenth century the widening of the social difference between capitalist and laborer had become more pronounced. As technology and industrialization progressed, factories went underground and with them their workers, who in time became adapted to the subterranean life and no longer came out into the light of day. (As we will see, the beginning of this process in the twenty-second century is later portrayed by Wells in the complementary stories, *When the Sleeper Wakes* and "A Story of the Days To Come.") Above ground the Haves pursued pleasure, comfort, and beauty; below ground the Have-Nots became continually adapted to the conditions of their labor. While the upper-worlders drifted to physical and mental ineffectiveness, the lower-worlders drifted to mere mechanical industry. However, since machines, no matter how perfect, require some intelligence to maintain, the Morlocks managed to retain some of their original intellectual strength, and, when the process of feeding the underworld became disrupted, the cosmic process reasserted itself and the Morlocks emerged to eat the Eloi. The world of 802,701 presents Huxley's trajectory of evolution some distance past the highest point, but still far from the end.

Escaping from the Morlocks, the Time Traveler pushes the levers in the wrong direction and rushes off into the even more distant future. The hand marking a thousand years sweeps by like the second hand on a watch, and he sees the earth nearing the end of the falling portion of Huxley's trajectory of evolution, thus bringing us to the idea which haunted Wells, Huxley, and others at the end of the nineteenth century—the death of our world.

No better introduction to late nineteenth- and early twentieth-century preoccupation with the end of the world exists than the history of the Second Law of Thermodynamics given by Henry Adams in *The Degradation of the Democratic Dogma*:

> Towards the middle of the nineteenth century,—that is, about 1850,—a new school of physicists appeared in Europe, dating from an Essay on the Motive Power of Heat, published by Sadi Carnot in 1824, and made famous by the names of William Thomson, Lord Kelvin, in England, and of Clausius and Helmholtz in Germany, who announced a second law of dynamics. The first law said that Energy was never lost; the second said that it was never saved; that, while the sum of energy in the universe might remain constant, —granting that the universe was a closed box from which nothing could escape,—the higher powers of energy tended always to fall lower, and that this process had no known limit.[21]

The Second Law led to a preoccupation with the end of the world because it showed that the dissipation of energy was a one-way process and that, as a result, a time would come when the earth was unfit for life.

And so it is that, as the Time Traveler drives on into the future, peculiar changes come over the earth. Day and night become longer, the sun moves more and more slowly across the sky. The great sun itself is changing, passing through an evolution in which its color becomes redder as it cools, while the moon has disappeared. At one point the Time Traveler stops his machine to look at our dying world—"the picture of this lethargic dying world," wrote Norman Nicholson, "is among the most significant passages in the popular literature of the last sixty years." [22] The air is much thinner. To the northeast the sky is black and the stars shine brilliantly; overhead the sky is a deep Indian red, merging into glowing scarlet to the south east. Along the southeastern horizon lies the huge red ball of the sun. Bright green lichenous plants grow everywhere and giant crab-like creatures crawl across the stony beach. Man has disappeared from the face of the earth. Fascinated by the earth's fate, the Time Traveler moves on into the future, and, at a point thirty million years hence, he sees the last signs of life on the dying earth. Although the huge sun now obscures nearly a tenth of the heavens, the air is bitter cold and snow is falling. Gone are the gigantic crab-like creatures, and the only signs of life are the livid green liverworts and lichens. Finally the Traveler sees the last animated creature, a round thing the size of a football trailing tentacles against the blood-red water. In horror he starts his machine and flees back to the comfortable present of his London home.

It is hard to exaggerate the significance of *The Time Machine.* Although Bellamy's *Looking Backward,* as Chad Walsh has said,[23] inspired a great number of dystopias like Konrad Wilbrandt's *Mr. East's Experiences in Mr. Bellamy's World* and Richard C. Michaelis's *Looking Forward,* which show the evils of a socialist future, their impact was slight since all were trivial as works of art. In the 1880's or

1890's the only vivid pictures of the future—besides Wells's —were utopias or utopian romances: *Looking Backward, News from Nowhere,* and *A Crystal Age. The Time Machine* was thus the first well-executed, imaginatively coherent picture of a future worse than the present, a picture at the same time generally anti-utopian in its tendencies. Indeed, in imaginative qualities it excels later anti-utopias, such as even *We* and *Brave New World,* being both more successful in domesticating the incredible and more poetic in its conception. Its coherence and power explain why it not only contributed numerous details and images to twentieth-century anti-utopias but made available to the literary consciousness a new form (science fiction) and suggested one use for this form (the attack on utopia).

IV

Wells's second scientific romance, *The Island of Dr. Moreau* (1896), is likewise brilliant, and likewise an influence on later anti-utopias. It is susceptible to careful analysis, both as to meaning and technique, but any such necessarily lengthy analysis would be irrelevant to the chief concerns of this book. Instead, I must refer the reader to the pertinent sections in the studies by Bernard Bergonzi, Geoffrey West, or Norman Nicholson, and regretfully limit myself only to what helps to explain the story's relationship to later anti-utopias.

The story begins with the promise of the horrible but still untold truth about a well-known shipwreck:

> I do not propose to add anything to what has already been written concerning the loss of the *Lady Vain.* As everyone knows, she collided with a derelict when ten days out from Callao. The long-boat with seven of the crew was picked up eighteen days after by H. M. gun-boat *Myrtle,* and the story of their privations has become almost

as well known as the far more terrible *Medusa* case. I have now, however, to add to the published story of the *Lady Vain* another as horrible, and certainly far stranger. (*IsM* 79)

And so Prendrick, the narrator, begins his "true account" of the events following the shipwreck, leading finally after incidents of hardship, treachery, and violence to his arrival on the island. Wells thus makes effective use of two devices once much employed to achieve plausibility in tales of extraordinary adventure: the first-person narrator and the imaginary voyage in the manner of Defoe's *Robinson Crusoe* and Swift's *Gulliver's Travels*.

By the time Prendrick is brought to the island, the reader is far along in his preparation for the revelation of Moreau's sinister activities. Wells completes the job with a few skillfully chosen details, such as the men in the boat that comes to get Prendrick—brown men whose "limbs were oddly swathed in some thin, dirty white stuff down even to the fingers and feet"; Prendrick's gradual recollection of the experiments in vivisection which had been called "The Moreau Horrors"; "something bound painfully upon a framework, scarred, red, and bandaged"; and screams sounding "as if all the pain in the world had found a voice." "Could the vivisection of men be possible?" Prendrick asks, and then flees. Eventually he is forced to parley with Moreau and learn the truth—which is that Moreau makes not animals out of men, but men out of animals, by surgery, chemical alteration of the blood, and hypnotism—but this not before Prendrick, having fallen in with the Beast People, witnesses, in one of the most effective scenes in the novel, the saying of the law. In a dark hut, swaying around a glimmer of fire, the Beast People chant:

"Not to go on all-Fours; *that* is the Law.
Are we not Men?"

"Not to suck up Drink; *that* is the Law.
Are we not Men?"

"Not to eat Flesh or Fish; *that* is the Law.
Are we not Men?"

"Not to claw Bark of Trees; *that* is the Law.
Are we not Men?"

"Not to chase other Men; *that* is the Law.
Are we not men?" (*IsM* 121)

Not long after Prendrick learns the truth about the island, Moreau's utopia begins to disintegrate. The doctor and his assistant are killed, the boats and supplies are destroyed, so that to survive Prendrick is forced to take his place among the Beast People. During ten ever more dangerous months he tries to rule them while they slowly slip back into the animal. At last, when the situation is desperate and Prendrick has no hope of continuing to defend himself, a boat with a sail drifts ashore—appropriately enough for such a novel, with two dead men in it: "dead so long that they fell to pieces when I tilted the boat on its side and dragged them out." And so Prendrick escapes.

A story that keeps the reader spellbound in terror, *The Island of Dr. Moreau* is also deeply pessimistic: as Norman Nicholson remarked, "no other novel of Wells is so completely hopeless." [24] *The Island of Dr. Moreau* takes T. H. Huxley's cosmic pessimism to its ultimate, saying not only that the evolutionary or cosmic process is savage and cruel and senseless and can never lead to ethical or social progress but that civilization is only a thin disguise hiding the fact that man is essentially bestial in nature, himself a product of the cosmic process. Indeed, says Wells, so much is man a part of the cosmic process that the beast in him threatens to break out at any time. *The Island of Dr. Moreau* is a parable of the cruelty, savagery, and arbitrariness of the cosmic process as it has created man and determined his nature.

This reading of the novel is consistent, too, with the interpretation, frequent since the earliest reviews, of Dr. Moreau as a caricature—most often a "blasphemous" caricature—of God. Certainly Wells used Moreau to caricature God, but, as Bergonzi noted, this is "not the traditional God of Christian theology, but the sort of arbitrary and impersonal power that might be conceived of as lying behind the evolutionary process." [25]

The richness of meaning of *The Island of Dr. Moreau* is not, of course, limited to the central theme that man is a part and product of the cruel and arbitrary cosmic process. Dr. Moreau, as Bergonzi pointed out, is also a symbol of "science unhindered by ethical considerations." [26] He is clearly not, however, Frankenstein the alchemist, as Bergonzi went on to suggest. Moreau's interest in knowledge for its own sake and faith in the scientific method are at the opposite pole from the alchemical-Frankenstein interest in science as a kind of magic to get something for nothing. Moreau is a far more sinister creature than the medieval Faust or Mary Shelley's Frankenstein. He has Huxley's intelligence, knowledge, and command of the powerful scientific method; but he does not have Huxley's controlling humanity. What we have here, of course, is a foreshadowing of the ruler of the modern scientific state.

Indeed, *The Island of Dr. Moreau* is very much in the stream of the anti-utopian tradition, for we can see emerging from this scientific romance, which is such a horrifying mixture of *Robinsonade* and Huxleyan pessimism, certain key details of later anti-utopias. Thus Moreau's activities foreshadow anti-utopian nightmare states whose rulers, free of all ethical considerations, employ biological, chemical, and psychological conditioning and manipulation in order to maintain total control over their citizens. And the chanting of the law of the Beast People foreshadows such ceremonies as the Day of Unanimity in *We*, the Soma Solidarity Service in *Brave New World*, and the Two-Minutes Hate in *Nineteen Eighty-four*. And, of course, in its inverted use of the desert island myth, *The Island of Dr. Moreau* looks forward to an important variant on the anti-utopian theme, William Golding's *Lord of the Flies*. But most of all it foreshadows later anti-utopias in its mood of hopelessness.

V

In connection with *The Island of Dr. Moreau*, I should mention *The Invisible Man* (1897), Wells's third scientific romance. In Griffin, the invisible man, we have the blood brother of Dr. Moreau: again, the scientist who has pursued knowledge and lost all human sympathy. But *The Invisible Man* is the closest of Wells's five great scientific romances to being a work of "sheer exuberance." Its serious meaning is almost completely "dissolved in the narrative" of the extraordinary adventures of the invisible man.

Wells's point of departure is, as usual, the everyday and familiar, only in this case it continues to be present in the foreground to a much greater extent than in the other scientific romances. The everyday and familiar is at first the sleepy and matter-of-fact Sussex village of Iping, to which Griffin comes to take up lodgings. His comic encounters with the villagers and others are handled with great skill, and in this respect the romance is a forerunner of Wells's masterpieces of lower-middle-class life, *Kipps* and *The History of Mr. Polly*. Altogether it is a greatly entertaining book, and chiefly a brilliant effervescence of the creative imagination.

Yet there are darker meanings within the narrative. Most obviously, in the ruthlessness of Griffin, who will rob and kill rather than have his wishes frustrated, we see illustrated, as

Wells himself tells us, "the dangers of power without control, the development of the intelligence at the expense of human sympathy." [27] Like *The Island of Dr. Moreau*, *The Invisible Man* thus foreshadows a major anti-utopian theme: the need for ethical control over the use of science and its discoveries. And how perfect a symbol of a science without humanity is an invisible man without scruples!

IN THE NEXT group of scientific romances, Wells's Huxleyan pessimism led him to move from the predominantly mythic technique of *The Time Machine* and *The Island of Dr. Moreau* to a much more satiric technique. The emergence of the twentieth-century anti-utopia was accelerated. The works in this group are *When the Sleeper Wakes*, "A Story of the Days To Come," and an obscure but related story, "A Dream of Armageddon," all three of which portray the same world of the twenty-second century; and *The First Men in the Moon*.

Striking similarities exist between Wells's picture of the twenty-second century and later anti-utopias, as, of course, George Orwell himself pointed out, and indeed the two stories in this list probably generate more anti-utopian images and ideas than any other of Wells's scientific romances, with the possible exception of *The First Men in the Moon*. All three works about the twenty-second century relate to the Socialist ferment and labor unrest of the 1890's, for they direct strong criticism against the evils wrought by capitalism, most dramatically its oppression of the urban proletariat, the people in what C. F. G. Masterman three years later called the Abyss.[1] Wells's chief method of criticism was to extrapolate from present conditions the development of capitalism and its effect on human life after two hundred years of ever accelerating scientific and technological progress, as he explained years afterwards in his *Experiment in Autobiography*:

> . . . the future in *When the Sleeper Wakes* was essentially an exaggeration of contemporary tendencies: higher buildings, bigger towns, wickeder capitalists and labour more downtrodden than ever and more desperate. Everything was bigger, quicker and more crowded; there was more and more flying and the wildest financial speculation. Very much the same picture is given in "A Story of the Days To Come" and "A Dream of Armageddon." [2]

The longest and by far the most important of these three is *When the Sleeper Wakes* (1899), and through it we can best approach Wells's idea of the nightmare world of the twenty-second century. Following Bellamy's device (the book can be considered a kind of answer to Bellamy), it tells how Graham, a Socialist of the "advanced school," falls into a trance in 1897 only to awaken in the spring of 2100. Not only does Graham discover that the world has changed beyond recognition—a subject we will discuss in detail in a moment—but he learns that he has become half-owner of the world because of the accumulation through two hundred years of investments left to him. A council of twelve able men have for many years ruled the world in Graham's name, but his awakening is the signal for a revolt against these trustees by the oppressed masses. Ostrog, the leader of the rebellion, does not, however, believe in human equality and is not interested in the welfare of the workers, and at the end Graham, in an effort to emancipate the workers, takes over the leadership of the rebellion. Single-handedly Graham forestalls the landing of Ostrog's African police, who come to suppress the masses; but whether the rebellion will be ultimately successful is not clear. This action is a prototype of the abortive rebellion which is such a key incident in most modern anti-utopias.

The darkness of the world in the twenty-second century is especially apparent to Graham, who awakes in the future still believing, as a nineteenth-century liberal, that "the sacrifice of the many to the few would some day cease, that a day was near when every child born of woman should have a fair and assured chance of happiness." Instead he finds that history has taken a much different course than Socialists like himself had expected. Because of "the moral decay that had followed the collapse of supernatural religion," the "decline of public honour," and the ascendancy of wealth, it had been a natural evolution of affairs during the period 1900–2100 for political power to fall into the hands of the small group of extremely able "bosses" who, in Graham's name, literally own the world and are so secure in their control that they have even thrown off the pretence of democracy and rule ruthlessly with the help of such enforcement agencies as the Labour Police. It is an amoral, materialistic society, consisting, beneath the bosses, of first a dwindling "middle class" of thoughtless, irresponsible seekers after sensation and pleasure, the minor rich and petty officials as well as "foremen, managers, the medical, legal, artistic and scholastic classes." Beneath this middle class lies the great mass of the population, ever increasing in numbers, the blue-uniformed slave workers of the Labour Company—"anaemic millions" crushed by the complexity of machine civilization, everywhere displaying "pale features, lean limbs, disfigurement and degeneration."

When the Sleeper Wakes, along with "A Story of the Days To Come," is memorable for the images and symbols it creates in describing the world of 2100. These are in most cases images and symbols generated completely or in part within the form itself, that is, science fiction. The first and most important of these is the "super city," which, as Richard Gerber notes, is the symbol in much twentieth-century utopian fantasy of "the interdependence of science, technology, industrialization, mass population, and social organization." [3] The chief source of this image of the super city in twentieth-century utopian fantasy is most likely Wells's picture of the inhumanly vast, complex mechanical anthill cities in which people live in the world of this novel and these two stories.

Our most important impression of the city comes shortly after Graham awakens from his sleep of 203 years and walks out on a balcony to see the titanic city for the first time. He is stunned as he looks at it through nineteenth-century eyes: [4]

His first impression was of overwhelming architecture. The place into which he looked was an aisle of Titanic buildings, curving spaciously in either direction. Overhead mighty cantilevers sprang together across the huge width of the place, and a tracery of translucent material shut out the sky. Gigantic globes of cool white light shamed the pale sunbeams that filtered down through the girders and wires. Here and there a gossamer suspension bridge dotted with foot passengers flung across the chasm and the air was webbed with slender cables. A cliff of edifice hung above him, he perceived as he glanced upward, and the opposite façade was grey and dim and broken by great archings, circular perforations, balconies, buttresses, turret projections, myriads of vast windows, and an intricate scheme of architectural relief. (WSW 28)

Then looking down he discovers beneath the balcony a colossal moving roadway:

... an endless flow rushing along as fast as a nineteenth-century express train, an endless platform of narrow transverse overlapping slats with little interspaces that permitted it to follow the curvatures of the street. Upon it were seats, and here and there little kiosks. ... (WSW 29)

Gradually Graham learns the patterns of this and similar cities. This particular giant is London, with a population of thirty-three million; and there are only four others in Britain—Edinburgh, Portsmouth, Manchester, and Shrewsbury. Like the others, it is a gigantic glass hive, an enormous Crystal Palace: all the city roadways, all the public squares and places, are covered in with glass as a protection against the weather; so that the roofing of London is practically continuous. On the roofs are landing stages for aircraft and giant windmills for generating power, "huge metallic structures, iron girders, inhumanly vast." And then the city ends abruptly in a wall: "a cliff, a steep fall of three or four hundred feet, a frontage broken only by terraces here and there, a complex decorative facade." (A few years later in *Anticipations* [1902] he was to change his prediction and see the city of the future as suburban sprawl rather than roofed-in metropolis.)

Outside the wall lies the uninhabited countryside, now tilled by the Food Company with great machines:

All about the city spread the carrot, swede [rutabaga], and turnip fields of the Food Company, vegetables that were the basis of a thousand varied foods, and weeds and hedgerow tangles had been utterly extirpated. The incessant expense of weeding that went on year after year in the petty, wasteful and barbaric farming of the ancient days, the Food Company had economised for ever more by a campaign of extermination. Here and there, however, neat rows of bramble standards and apple trees with whitewashed stems, intersected the fields, and at places groups of gigantic teazles reared their favoured spikes.

Here and there huge agricultural machines hunched under water-proof covers. The mingled waters of the Wey and Mole and Wandle ran in rectangular channels; and wherever a gentle elevation of the ground permitted a fountain of deodorised sewage distributed benefits athwart the land and made a rainbow of the sunlight. (WSW 212)

And scattered here and there are the overgrown ruins of deserted villages, towns, and suburbs.

The idea of the inhumanly vast giant city in its turn gives birth to several major clusters of subordinate images, clusters which are themselves often repeated in later anti-utopian fiction. Thus, for example, Graham discovers that the private household has disappeared:

In this matter, for instance, it had not occurred to him that this continuity of the city, this exclusion of weather, these vast halls and ways, involved the disappearance of the household; that the typical Victorian "Home," the little brick cell containing kitchen and scullery, living rooms and bedrooms, had, save for the ruins that diversified the countryside, vanished as surely as the wattle hut. But now he saw what had indeed been manifest from the first, that London, regarded as a living place, was no longer an aggregation of houses but a prodigious hotel, an hotel with a thousand classes of accommodation, thousands of dining halls, chapels, theatres, markets and places of assembly, a synthesis of enterprises, of which he chiefly was the owner. People had their sleeping rooms, with, it might be antechambers, rooms that were always sanitary at least whatever the degree of comfort and privacy, and for the rest they lived much as many people had lived in the new-made giant hotels of the Victorian days, eating, reading, thinking, playing, conversing, all in places of public resort, going to their work in the industrial quarters of the city or doing business in their offices in the trading section. (WSW 141)

And he naturally learns that these people eat in vast common dining halls, Wells's modification of an old idea in utopian literature. The tables are very different from those of Victorian times:

There were no ornaments, no flowers, and the table was without a cloth, being made, he learnt, of a solid substance having the texture and appearance of damask. He discerned that this damask substance was patterned with gracefully designed trade advertisements. (WSW 143)

And along the upper walls huge advertisement dioramas move majestically.

Naturally, with the dissolution of the private household goes the dissolution of the family, so that most parents pack their children off to crèches and Child Educational Refineries, a variation on another familiar utopian idea. The theme of the inhumanly vast and the mechanical is continued in the description of these institutions. Thus the mechanical arrangement for the care of babies in glass enclosed boxes is suggestive of modern incubators or the Skinner box:

Elaborate apparatus watched the atmosphere and rang a bell far away in the central office at the slightest departure from the optimum of temperature and moisture. A system of such crèches had almost entirely replaced the hazardous adventures of the old-world nursing. The attendant presently called Graham's attention to the wet nurses, a vista of mechanical figures, with arms, shoulders, and breasts of astonishingly realistic modelling, articulation, and texture, but mere brass tripods below, and having in the place of features a flat disc bearing advertisements likely to be of interest to mothers. (WSW 146)

Another rich and important cluster of images describes the Labour Company, whose servants and debtors include nearly a third of the population of the world—from the cradle to the grave. Its origin is described with the kind of satiric inversion common to later anti-utopias:

The Labour Company ousted the workhouse. It grew—partly—out of something—you, perhaps, may remember it—an emotional organisation called the Salvation Army—that became a business company. In the first place it was almost a charity. To save people from workhouse rigours. Now I come to think of it, it was one of the earliest properties your Trustees acquired. They bought the Salvation Army and reconstructed it. . . . (WSW 130)

They reconstructed it as a vast organization providing all but the very highest and most responsible labor throughout the world. Its workers, who wear blue canvas uniforms, receive food, shelter, and a few pence inducement to effort, but once they have donned blue canvas they are almost never able to break away. Even their children are caught, being converted by psychological conditioning "into beautifully punctual and trustworthy machine minders." And gradually these workers are differentiating into a distinct race, with moral and physical differences of its own—even with a crude thick dialect of its own. It is very evident that these workers evolve into the Morlocks of 802,701, especially when we learn that they labor in subterranean factories.

Indeed, one of the sections most anti-utopian in the twentieth-century sense in these altogether frightening works is Chapter XXI, "The Under Side," of *When the Sleeper Wakes*. Here Wells describes Graham's visit to the underground factories manned by blue-clad workers, who work in dust and darkness, minding machines, becoming pale and disfigured by their labor. It is presented in a series of images of great vividness: pinched faces, feeble muscles, livid white lips and nostrils, racking coughs—and the Labour Police, armed with clubs, trotting toward some unknown disturbance. Not only does this reach back to *The Time Machine*, but it looks forward to the Gammas, Deltas, and Epsilons of Huxley's *Brave New World* and the proles of Orwell's *Nineteen Eighty-four*.

But there are many other, smaller details which are to reappear in twentieth-century anti-utopias, details which result from the fact that these works are, after all, science fiction. The Sanitary Company burns books to make *ashlarite* while the people watch kineto-tele-photographs— our television—or listen to phonograph lectures (thus Wells anticipates the central idea of Ray Bradbury's anti-utopia, *Fahrenheit 451*). In the streets and public ways great Babble Machines blare forth news and propaganda:

The Master [Graham] is sleeping peacefully. . . . He is in excellent health. He is going to devote the rest of his life to aeronautics. He says women are more beautiful than ever. Galloop! Wow! Our wonderful civilisation astonishes him beyond measure. Beyond all measure. Galloop. He puts great trust in Boss Ostrog, absolute confidence in Boss Ostrog. Ostrog is to be his chief minister; is authorized to remove or reinstate public officers—all patronage will be in his hands. All patronage in the hands of Boss Ostrog! (*WSW* 143)

And factories exist where feverishly competitive authors devise their phonograph lectures and advertisements. Then there are the Pleasure Cities, suggestive of the sex and soma of *Brave New World*: "Strange places reminiscent of the legendary Sybaris, cities of art and beauty, mercenary art and mercenary beauty, sterile wonderful cities of motion and music, whither repaired all who profited by the fierce, inglorious, economic struggle that went on in the glaring labyrinth below" (p. 96). And for those who can afford it, there is Euthanasy, the easy death, and to forget the unpleasant, there is psychic surgery, performed by hypnosis. Hypnosis is also an important part of the educational process.

At times Wells is brilliantly satiric in the manner of such post-World War II magazine science fiction as *The Space Merchants*. Thus Graham travels into the religious quarter and sees the façade of one of the Christian sects "covered with inscriptions from top to base, in vivid white and blue, save where a vast and glaring kinematograph transparency presented a realistic New Testament scene." He is appalled by the incredible blasphemy of the inscriptions:

"Salvation on the First Floor and turn to the Right." "Put your Money on your Maker." "The Sharpest Conversions in London, Expert Operators! Look Slippy." "What Christ would say to the Sleeper—Join the Up-to-date Saints!" "Be a Christian—without hindrance to your present Occupation." "All the Brightest Bishops on the Bench to-night and Prices as Usual." "Brisk Blessings for Busy Business Men." (WSW 140)

This world of the twenty-second century is also the world in which the action in "A Story of the Days To Come" (1897) is set, and it is a distant background for "A Dream of Armageddon." In "A Story of the Days To Come," the love of the two central characters, Elizabeth and Denton, is contrasted with the oppressive tyranny of life in the super-city, and as such it looks forward to all the love affairs in subsequent anti-utopias. And at one point, in an incident rich in significance for later anti-utopias, Elizabeth and Denton attempt to escape to freedom outside the wall. Carrying food supplies, they go into the ruined countryside. They are told by a worker there of a place among the ruins where they might find shelter, though he warns them:

"But it's a quiet place. There is no light after dark there, and I have heard tell of robbers. It is lonely. Nothing happens there. The phonographs of the story-tellers, the kinematograph entertainments, the new machines—none of them are to be found there. If you are hungry there is no food, if you are ill no doctor. . . ." He stopped.
"We shall try it," said Denton, moving to go on. Then a thought struck him, and he made an agreement with the shepherd, and learnt where they might find him, to buy and bring them anything of which they stood in need, out of the city.
And in the evening they came to the deserted village, with its houses that seemed so small and odd to them: they found it golden in the glory of the sunset, and desolate and still. They went from one

deserted house to another, marvelling at their quaint simplicity, and debating which they should choose. And at last, in a sunlit corner of a room that had lost its outer wall, they came upon a wild flower, a little flower of blue that the weeders of the Food Company had over-looked. (*WSW* 215)

And so they spend their first night outside the city, to awake in the morning to the sound of a thrush, surely the same thrush that sings to Julia and Winston in *Nineteen Eighty-four*. But in the next few days, they are attacked by wild dogs and so driven back to the city, having been made too soft by mechanical civilization to survive outside it.

An apocalyptic glare is thrown over this nightmare world of the twenty-second century in "A Dream of Armageddon" (1901), a vivid story dealing with the coming of a cataclysmic war to this world as it is witnessed from Capri and Italy by a leader who has relinquished his power, power which could have averted the very disaster that engulfs him and his mistress. The story is directly related to *When the Sleeper Wakes* and "A Story of the Days To Come" since Capri is one of the Pleasure Cities of the twenty-second century. In its description of a cataclysmic war, the story looks forward to Wells's future histories that will describe the war and collapse of civilization preceding the founding of the great World State.

II

There can be no question, of course, that as a story *The First Men in the Moon* (1901) is one of Wells's best (he thought it was his best), but it is also one of Wells's most serious comments on human life in a mechanical and scientific age. What it represents, in terms of our subject, is the Wellsian scientific romance nearly transformed into the modern anti-utopia, and as such it is very similar to the stories about the twenty-second century which we have just discussed. It differs, however, from Wells's stories of the twenty-second century as well as from the modern anti-utopias in that it returns to the techniques, employed so skillfully in *The Time Machine* and *The Island of Dr. Moreau*, for domesticating the incredible.

In *The First Men in the Moon*, two Englishmen, Bedford and Cavor, travel to our satellite in a sphere coated with the antigravity substance, Cavorite. There they are captured by the Selenites, who carry the two men into the caverns beneath the moon's surface. Bedford escapes and returns alone to the earth while Cavor is taken into the interior of the moon, where he observes the tremendously specialized lunar society and for a time is able to send back reports by wireless to the earth before the Selenites silence him forever. It is a brilliant story in which Wells first prepares for the journey to the moon by creating the two characters, Bedford and Cavor; placing them in a solid earthly environment; and then, when the reader's scepticism has been lulled, introducing the miraculous Cavorite.[5]

The First Men in the Moon is, of course, a classic example of a very old genre, the cosmic voyage, whose defining conventions were established in the seventeenth century under the impact of the new astronomy. Although Wells knows and uses the whole tradition, his most important indebtedness, as Coleman Parsons and Marjorie Nicolson have shown, is to the conception of the moon in Kepler's *Somnium* [6]— a porous moon with great caverns in which the lunar creatures hide from the extremes of temperatures, with the so-called craters as entrances to the world inside. But Wells forges this anew in the furnace of his imagination, and indeed he takes most of the old conventions of the cosmic voyage and infuses them with a new poetic vitality. This is apparent in the narrative of the beautiful, silent journey through star-dusted space and the landing on the moon at the dawn of a lunar day. Wells's imagination is also evident in the description of the moon's interior, with its blue-lit passageways and tunnels lying above the great swirling, luminescent central sea that laps around the lunar core.

We have been so caught up in the journey through space and the landing on the moon that we are now ready to accept Wells's description of the civilization of the Selenites, his vivid picture of the great anthill which is the interior of the moon. The idea of the Selenites as ants, albeit intelligent, and the moon as an anthill is a brilliant foreshadowing of the giant World States of twentieth-century anti-utopias.

One implied criticism of human life in *The First Men in the Moon* is a paradox of the twentieth century which Wells presents but cannot resolve: how, in an age of science and technology, can the world achieve economic, social, political stability and efficiency and, at the same time, not dehumanize the individual by completely controlling him? Wells describes here the ultimate in "specialization," a word which means in the context of the book the thorough adaptation of the organism to its function in society.

"In the moon," Cavor observes, "every citizen knows his place. He is born to that place, and the elaborate discipline of training and education and surgery he undergoes fits him at last so completely to it that he has neither ideas nor organs for any purpose beyond it" (p. 601). And so the moon is a forerunner of the twentieth-century *Brave New World*, a state in which each individual is, by physical, psychological, and chemical means, irresistibly adapted to his position and even comes to hate those who are not like him. Thus the description of the lunar artist:

Eat little—drink little—draw. Love draw. No other thing. Hate all who do not draw like him. Angry. Hate all who draw better. Hate most people. Hate all who not think all world for to draw. Angry. M'm. All things mean nothing to him—only draw. (*FMM* 600)

In its division into classes, it suggests the division in twentieth-century anti-utopias—and like them mocks the division which Plato thought necessary and which Wells, in later writings such as *A Modern Utopia*, thought necessary. Thus, although there are as many different kinds of Selenites as there are different kinds of work to be performed, all lunar society can be divided into two broad categories, the intellectual classes and the workers. Within the intellectual classes there are three groups, all equipped with enlarged brain cases. (In this respect they hark back to the Martians in *The War of the Worlds* as well as look forward to Wells's later concern with limitations imposed by the size of man's brain case.) The first class, the administrators such as Phi-oo, who takes Cavor in charge, are responsible for certain regions of the moon and are characterized by the greatest diversity of talents. The experts, with their gigantic balloon-shaped brains, are created to perform special mental operations. The learned, such as Tsi-puff, the first lunar professor of terrestrial languages, are the receptacles of knowledge, and so great is their power that they replace books, libraries, and museums. The rest of lunar society is made up of the workers, whose forms are as numerous as there are jobs to be filled: glass blowers who are all lungs; chemists who are only a great arm and quick eyes; vigorous guards and soldiers; miniature Selenites to do fine, precision work; spidery messengers; stocky butchers with long arms; workers who are all hands to assemble machinery; living lanterns, and many, many others. When one of these workers is no longer needed, he is drugged into suspended animation until his services are again required.

The great anthill of the moon is cruel, inhuman, and even the scientist Cavor, who can rationally understand the reasons for it, is shocked when he comes upon young Selenites, "confined in jars from which only the forelimbs protruded, who were being compressed to become machine-minders of a special sort." The memory of these "extended hands" haunts him, and, yet, he wonders ironically if it is not "really in the end a more humane proceeding than our earthly method of leaving children to grow into human beings, and then making machines of them" (p. 604).

At the same time that the reader is made to reject the Selenite's ruthless adaptation of the individual so that he may efficiently carry out his function, he is also invited to admire what results from this adaptation: a World State intelligently mobilized to employ all knowledge for the most efficient utilization of the planet's resources. Wells's admiration of the end—as distinguished from the means—is most apparent in Cavor's interview with the Grand Lunar, apparently modeled after Gulliver's audience with the King of Brobdingnag, in which the disorder and chaos of earthly life is ruthlessly satirized.

Just as Gulliver's glowing account of the accomplishments and history of England and Europe reveal more than he intends, so Cavor's description of the earth, its inhabitants, and their culture brings forth only amazement and ridicule from the Grand Lunar. The absolute ruler of the moon cannot, of course, understand Cavor's explanation of the "democratic method" and asks him to repeat it, thinking something has gone wrong in translation—Wells had already come to distrust democracy, as we can see in *Anticipations* and *A Modern Utopia*. And, of course, Cavor's description of war shocks the Grand Lunar. "You mean to say," the Grand Lunar asks, "that you run over the surface of your world—this world whose riches you have scarcely begun to scrape—killing one another for beasts to eat?" (p. 617) Too late, Cavor realizes that his indiscreet revelations have jeopardized his own safety. After the interview, his wireless transmissions are at first intermittently jammed and then finally ended entirely, presumably with his death. He is never able to send to earth the formula for the manufacture of Cavorite, and the Selenites thus at least postpone for many years, perhaps centuries, further visits to the moon of the unpleasant race of men.

But there is yet another meaning, without question embedded in the story though hardly as close to the surface as the problem of stability vs. freedom. This is to say, *The First Men in the Moon* is again a parable of what science can do, and the Selenites and their civilization symbolize the frightening power of coming inventions and discoveries to overturn completely the old order, just as do the Martians in *The War of the Worlds*. This meaning is given direct expression by Bedford himself at one point where he comments on the significance of the wireless messages from Cavor inside the moon:

This intermittent trickle of messages, this whispering of a record needle in the darkness of the mountain slopes, is the first warning of such a change in human conditions as mankind has scarcely imagined heretofore. In that planet there are new elements, new appliances, new traditions, an overwhelming avalanche of ideas. . . . (*FMM* 607)

S OMETIME near the end of the 1890's, Wells began to occupy himself more directly and specifically with social, economic, and political problems and so entered on the path that led to his becoming the twentieth century's foremost writer of utopias. He continued to believe that the greatest enemy of progress was faith in inevitable progress, but he turned from shocking men out of their complacency to holding out ideas toward which they should strive. Eventually his concern with human welfare produced what Mencken in 1919 called his "Messianic delusion" [1] and a consequent decline in artistic quality as he increasingly subordinated delight to instruction—in all his writings, fiction and non-fiction, utopias and regular novels. Wells's sense of mission and his shift to journalism and propaganda helped to alienate those who, responding to the new cultural movement which rejected science, progress, and faith in man's perfectibility, embraced anti-utopianism. The hero of the first two decades of the century became the symbol of everything most intellectuals hated, and his vision of utopia the object of scorn. At first consciously, then unconsciously, the anti-utopians attacked this vision, and ironically, they used as a vehicle Wellsian science fiction, at the same time borrowing numerous details from such stories as *The Time Machine, The Island of Dr. Moreau, When the Sleeper Wakes* and "A Story of the Days To Come," and *The First Men in the Moon.*

But in attacking the Wellsian utopia, the major anti-utopias are greatly indebted to it since much of their attack consists of parody and caricature. The explanation of what Wells was attempting to do when he wrote utopias is given in "The So-Called Science of Sociology," a paper he read to the Sociological Society in February, 1906, and which was later reprinted in *An Englishman Looks at the World.*

In "The So-Called Science of Sociology," Wells denied that Herbert Spencer and Comte had created a new and fruitful system of human inquiry, denied that a science of sociology is possible. This assertion was based on Wells's belief in the uniqueness of everything in the universe and the impossibility of dealing with people in sufficiently large numbers to make the kind of generalizations, say, that physicists can make about atoms:

If we quite boldly face the fact that hard positive methods are less and less successful just in proportion as our "ologies" deal with larger and less numerous individuals; if we admit that we become less "scientific" as we ascend the scale of the sciences, and that we do and must change our method, then it is humbly submitted, we shall be in a much better position to consider the question of "approaching" sociology. We shall realize that all this talk of the organisation of sociology, as though presently the sociologist would be going about the world with the authority of a sanitary engineer, is and will remain nonsense.[2]

Instead, sociology "must be neither art simply, nor science in the narrow meaning of the word at all, but knowledge rendered imaginatively, and with an element of personality; that is to say, in the highest sense of the term, literature."

Wells saw two chief literary forms as usefully serving sociological purposes. The first—the historical—he said, is invariably recognized as valuable. But it is the second—the utopian—which, although it is usually neglected, was to him more important: "I think, in fact, that the creation of Utopias—and their exhaustive criticism—is the proper and distinctive method of sociology." Wells called for an enormous amount of utopian speculation and criticism:

I figure to myself a similar book, a sort of dream book of huge dimensions, in reality perhaps dispersed in many volumes by many hands, upon the Ideal Society. This book, this picture of the perfect state, would be the backbone of sociology. It would have great sections devoted to such questions as the extent of the Ideal Society, its relation to racial differences, the relations of the sexes in it, its economic organisations, its organisation for thought and education, its "Bible"—as Dr. Beattie Crozier would say—its housing and social atmosphere, and so forth. Almost all the divaricating work at present roughly classed together as sociological could be brought into relation in the simplest manner, either as new suggestions, as new discussion or criticism, as newly ascertained facts bearing upon such discussions and sustaining or eliminating suggestions. The institutions of existing states would come into comparison with the institutions of the Ideal State, their failures and defects would be criticised most effectually in that relation, and the whole science of collective psychology, the psychology of human association, would be brought to bear upon the question of the practicability of this proposed ideal.[3]

To a very great extent, Wells devoted the rest of his life to writing—and criticizing—this dream book.

The Wellsian vision of utopia, so often attacked in the major anti-utopias, can also be found in whole or in part in certain of Wells's novels, like *The Passionate Friends* and *The Research Magnificent*, as well as in such expository works as *Anticipations*, *The Outline of History*, and *The Open Conspiracy*. But for the purposes of our discussion of this vision, it is best to rely chiefly on the utopias, since it is there we find the vision in its most concentrated form and, accordingly, there it is most likely to be the object of direct attack. Nor do we diminish Wells's accomplishment if we recognize that this vision represents an evolution of traditional utopian thought into an age of science and technology. It makes no difference that there are ideas in this vision which derive from the great utopias from Plato to More to Bellamy or that the vision can be seen in Winwood Reade's *The Martyrdom of Man*, a very Victorian book and a favorite of Wells's. It is not the originality of Wells's vision but its overwhelming vigor, vitality, and comprehensiveness that make it a chief target of twentieth-century anti-utopians. One should add, too, that, although Wells was not always consistent from book to book, one can still describe his vision in general terms. In fact, one can write the history of the rise of the Wellsian utopia and its evolution when once established. But before doing so we need first to look at basic assumptions underlying the Wellsian vision.

The first of these assumptions is one which we have seen Wells take from T. H. Huxley—the belief that the cosmic process is an amoral force which man must check if there is to be any human progress. Essentially, Wells, influenced by Huxley and also Darwin, came to believe that there is no inherent virtue in nature (in the sense of all physical reality, human and non-human) and that in order to better the human lot man must control, regulate, and transform nature. As we will see later, most of the anti-utopians tend to hold the quite antithetical view that man tampers with nature only at great risk since there is some kind of higher wisdom somewhere in the order of the universe—in God or in nature itself. Wells believed not only that man can but that he must improve on nature, and the standard by which improvements are to be judged is the welfare of the species. These opposing attitudes toward nature lead to the classic arguments for and against utopia, which are succinctly presented (as we will see later) in a debate in *Men Like Gods* between a visitor to Utopia, Rupert Catskill, and the Utopian host, Urthred.

It is no surprise, then, that in Wells's utopias men have taken to mastering nature, and thus a second assumption in the Wellsian vision, and a corollary of the first, is that science and technology are inherently good for man and can help to build a mighty future. The classic statement of this view, which we will discuss shortly, is in Wells's *A Modern Utopia* (1905).

At this point it is in order to describe Wells's favorite and most spectacular prediction as to how the great utopia will come into existence. In this prediction the world utopia is established after the collapse of civilization brought on by the cataclysmic wars that are the consequence of the continuation of old national rivalries in a world of new science and technology. With variations, this future history is narrated at length in *The War in the Air* (1908), *The World Set Free* (1914), and *The Shape of Things To Come* (1934). It is also at the core of the mythic meaning of *The War of the Worlds* (1898), in which the superior Martians, with their advanced science and technology, put human civilization to rout. The difference is that what is myth in *The War of the Worlds* becomes detailed and explicit prophecy in the three future histories. Needless to say, the Wellsian story of the end of civilization brought by a disastrous war (also indebted to the tradition of invasion stories begun with Chesney's "Battle of Dorking") is the most influential ancestor of the nuclear holocaust novels so popular in recent years. More important for us here, the Wellsian prediction is incorporated in many of the major anti-utopias, where world war and the collapse of civilization precede the creation of monstrous superstates.

Easily the best of Wells's three future histories is the first, *The War in the Air,* in which catastrophe begins with the surprise attack of the German air fleet on New York, turning that greatest of cities into a fiery holocaust. As the war spreads and the air fleets of the world tear themselves to pieces, the world's economic order collapses:

Above was visible conflict and destruction; below something was happening far more deadly and incurable to the flimsy fabric of finance and commercialism in which men had so blindly put their trust. As the airships fought above, the visible gold supply of the world vanished below. An epidemic of private cornering and universal distrust swept the world. In a few weeks, money, except for depreciated paper, vanished into vaults, into holes, into the walls of the houses, into ten million hidingplaces. Money vanished, and at its disappearance trade and industry came to an end. The economic world staggered and fell dead. It was like the stroke of some disease; it was like the water vanishing out of the blood of a living creature; it was a sudden universal coagulation of intercourse. . . . (WA 224)

And then, as an inevitable consequence, there follows universal social collapse:

Wherever there were great populations, great masses of people found themselves without work, without money, and unable to get food. Famine was in every working-class quarter in the world within three weeks of the beginning of the war. Within a month there was not a city anywhere in which the ordinary law and social procedure had not been replaced by some form of emergency control, in which firearms and military executions were not being used to keep order and prevent violence. And still in the poorer quarters, and in the populous districts, and even here and there already among those who had been wealthy, famine spread. (WA 225)

Finally comes rioting, the plague, and a return to semi-barbarism—every government in the world "shattered and broken as a heap of china beaten with a stick." *The War in the Air* is thus an early ancestor of the many stories in the twentieth century of man's primitive descendants, but, unlike Richard Jefferies's *After London* (1885), another influential story on the same theme and a protest against industrialism and "progress," it does not portray the end of civilization and the return to primitivism as a blessing:

The great nations and empires have become names in the mouths of men. Everywhere there are ruins and unburied dead, and shrunken, yellow-faced survivors in a mortal apathy. Here there are robbers, here vigilance committees, and here guerilla bands ruling patches of exhausted territory, strange federations and brotherhoods form and dissolve, and religious fanaticisms begotten of despair gleam in famine-bright eyes. It is a universal dissolution. (WA 226)

The creation of the world utopia which later rises from the ruins is only implied, for all we learn is that the book is supposedly written in a later era after order has been restored: "To men living in our present world state, orderly, scientific and secured, nothing seems so precarious, so giddily dangerous, as the fabric of the social order with which the men of the opening of the twentieth century were content" (p. 220).

Six years later, in *The World Set Free*, Wells again wrote of world disaster and the end of the old civilization, but the collapse is brought by the dropping of atomic bombs in a war between Russia, France, and England and the Central Powers of Europe. Much the same situation exists as in *The War in the Air*:

. . . the flimsy fabric of the world's credit had vanished, industry was completely disorganized and every city, every thickly populated area was starving or trembled on the verge of starvation. Most of the capital cities of the world were burning; millions of people had already perished, and over great areas government was at an end.[4]

But this time some of the leaders of the world's governments survive, eventually come to their senses, and meet together at Brissago in Italy to set about creating the modern World State.

This same pattern of future history leading to the World State, which Wells established in *The War in the Air* and *The World Set Free*, is repeated in *The Shape of Things To Come*, only at much greater length and much more elaborately. In fact this greater sophistication is one of the chief defects of the book. In its first four sections it is virtually unreadable because of the lumbering manner in which Wells recounts the devastation and disorder, and the world councils and their rules which usher in the new utopia; and because it is clotted with ideas which overwhelm the slight story line. Except for certain parts of the utopian fifth book, where Wells occasionally rises to his old levels of vitality, he has here almost entirely relinquished imaginative literature for exhortatory sociology. *The Shape of Things To Come* is manifestly the product of a tired imagination.

II

The Wellsian utopia itself, which often rises from the ruins of civilization when a functional elite of engineers, scientists, and professional men seize control of air power and form a world council, evolves through at least two stages. A utopia of the earliest stage is described in *A Modern Utopia* (1905), which is the first of the sort Wells wrote, and easily the finest. The book has considerable historical interest. It is very much a part of the social and economic unrest that in the General Election of 1906 brought the Liberal party to power with an overwhelming majority and gave Labour fifty-three seats; and it is intimately connected with the attempt of the still young and aggressive Wells to wrest control from

Shaw and the Webbs and turn the Fabian Society, as Wells explained later, "into the beginnings of an order, akin to these Samurai in A Modern Utopia, which should embody for mankind a sense of the state." [5] The attempt failed, and, wearied at last of brilliant debates which never resulted in action, Wells resigned from the Society in 1908, thereafter relying chiefly on his pen to bring into existence the New Republic, the great utopian World State.

The immediate impact of A Modern Utopia was enormous, and men like Henry James and Joseph Conrad were, as Geoffrey West said of Henry James, "abject in admiration." [6] James, impressed by the quality of mind displayed in A Modern Utopia, wrote, "Bravo, bravo, my dear Wells!" And Conrad praised the book for its "intellectual kindliness" in extending a hand to civilization. William James dashed off a note to tell Wells that he had "given a shove to the practical thought of the next generation" that would be among its greatest influences for good. [7] The book was widely reviewed, and treated with respect; and, though not everyone agreed with its proposals, most critics believed (as did Van Wyck Brooks ten years later) that it was "a beautiful utopia, beautifully seen and beautifully thought." It is, of course, central to the development of the utopian tradition in the twentieth century, [8] as is proven by its influence on B. F. Skinner's Walden Two, one of the most important utopias since Wells.

A Modern Utopia is perhaps, as Geoffrey West remarked, "the most characteristic—the most Wellsian—of all his books." [9] Part of this originality is in the form itself, which Wells arrived at after rejecting in turn the serious essay, the discussion novel in the manner of Peacock and Mallock, the Socratic dialogue, and the straight narrative. What Wells finally achieved was a kind of discussion novel without all the characters, "a sort of shot-silk texture between philosophical discussion on the one hand and imaginative narrative on the other" (p. xxxii).

Unlike *The War in the Air, The World Set Free,* and *The Shape of Things To Come,* the upheaval which precedes the establishment of Utopia is not described, and instead we are presented with Utopia as an accomplished fact. "By an act of the imagination" we are taken to this Utopia when the narrator and his companion descend from the Lucendro Pass into our world's physical duplicate, another planet circling another sun far out in the depths of space beyond Sirius: "It is a planet like our planet, the same continents, the same islands, the same oceans and seas, another Fuji-Yama is beautiful there dominating another Yokohama—and another Matterhorn overlooks the icy disorder of another Theodule" (p. 13).

Ideally, wrote Wells, we would change everything, making Utopia a golden country:

Were we free to have our untrammeled desire, I suppose we should follow Morris to his Nowhere, we should change the nature of man and the nature of things together; we should make the whole race wise, tolerant, noble, perfect—wave our hands to a splendid anarchy, every man doing as it pleases him, and none pleased to do evil, in a world as good in its essential nature, as ripe and sunny, as the world before the Fall. (*MU* 7)

But, Wells reluctantly continued, we must be limited by the possibilities of space and time, where the "pervading Will to Live sustains for ever more a perpetuity of aggressions." And so Wells restricted himself to men and women as we know them in our world today and nature in all its inhumanity and insubordination. Only the conditions of human life are changed:

. . . a free hand with all the apparatus of existence that man has, so to speak, made for himself, with houses, roads, clothing, canals, machinery, with laws, boundaries, conventions, and traditions, with schools, with literature and religious organisations, with creeds and customs, with everything, in fact, that it lies within man's power to alter. (*MU* 8)

And this, as Wells noted, is the cardinal assumption of all utopian speculations, old and new: "the Republic and Laws of Plato and More's Utopia, Howells' implicit Altruria, and Bellamy's future Boston, Comte's great Western Republic, Hertzka's Freeland, Cabet's Icaria, and Campanella's City of the Sun" (p. 8).

Wells's reference to many of the major works in the utopian tradition brings to mind Lewis Mumford's comments that *A Modern Utopia* is "the quintessential utopia," that in it Wells "sums up and clarifies the utopias of the past." [10] Indeed, in *A Modern Utopia* Wells wrote the archetypal utopia, brought up to date, with science and technology assimilated into it as never before. It becomes the utopia transformed into an archetypal blueprint for the scientifically planned welfare state, as well as an early major statement of Wells's dream of the World State. And altogether it is effective as the unique kind of fiction it sets out to be, while, at the same time, it is intellectually rigorous and hard. It is no wonder that utopian came to mean Wellsian for men like Forster, Huxley, and Orwell.

The most important feature of *A Modern Utopia*, and its greatest contribution to the literature of utopian thought, is its concept of utopia as planet-wide. Wells noted that once a mountain valley or an island offered sufficient isolation "for a polity to maintain itself intact from outward force," and he cited as examples Plato's *Republic*, Bacon's *New Atlantis*, and More's *Utopia*. Even works as recent as "Butler's satirical 'Erewhon,' and Mr. Stead's queendom of inverted sexual conditions in Central Africa, found the Tibetan method of slaughtering the inquiring visitor a simple, sufficient rule."

But all the force of modern conditions is against the permanence of such enclosures:

We are acutely aware nowadays that, however subtly contrived a State may be, outside your boundary lines the epidemic, the breeding barbarian or the economic power, will gather its strength to overcome you. The swift march of invention is all for the invader. Now, perhaps you might still guard a rocky coast or a narrow pass; but what of that near to-morrow when the flying machine soars overhead, free to descend at this point or that? A state powerful enough to keep isolated under modern conditions would be powerful enough to rule the world, would be, indeed, if not actively ruling, yet passively acquiescent in all other human organizations, and so responsible for them altogether. (*MU* 11)

A World State, then, Wells's modern utopia must be.

The second most important feature of *A Modern Utopia* is the class of *samurai*, an order of "voluntary nobility" which represents a reappearance, though greatly modified, of Plato's Guardians. "As it has developed in my mind," writes Wells's visitor to Utopia, "it has reminded me more and more closely of that strange class of guardians which constitutes the essential substance of Plato's *Republic*. . . ." (p. 259) Practically all the political power rests in their hands, for not only are they the only administrators, lawyers, practising doctors, and public officials of almost every sort, but they are also the only voters. They exist because Wells believed that the large intricacy of utopian organization demanded more powerful and efficient methods of control than the democratic process allowed. Wells had first described them in 1902 in *Anticipations* as the "New Republicans," and the Voice refers to the idea as coming from "a literary man" who "was a little vague in his proposals." This idea of a functional elite appears again and again in Wells's plans for the World State.

The order of the *samurai* is open to any adult over twenty-five, who is in a reasonably healthy and efficient state, and who has passed the exit examination in a college or upper school. If he joins the order, he must follow the "Rule," which forbids such things as alcohol, drugs, smoking, betting, usury, games, trade, and servants. He must wear the austere dress of the order and keep himself in good health and physical condition, and he must keep his mind alert by reading a certain number of new books a year. Chastity is required, but not celibacy, though if the *samurai* marries he can only remain in the order if his wife at least follows the woman's "Lesser Rule." Finally, each year he must spend at least seven consecutive days alone in a wild and solitary place, developing his inner resources. The Spartan quality of this regimen obviously derives from the life of Plato's Guardians.

The third most distinctive feature—and one which contributes greatly to making it a *modern* utopia—is the importance Wells assigns to science and technology. To a great extent the dream first dimly delineated in Bacon's *New Atlantis* has come true in *A Modern Utopia*. "Bacon's visionary House of Salomon will be a thing realized," and Utopian research goes "like an eagle's swoop in comparison with the blindman's fumbling of our terrestrial way" (p. 60). Wells's research institute is devoted to the same systematic development of science for the betterment of the human condition that Bacon proposed as the purpose of the House of Salomon: "The end of our foundation is the knowledge of causes, and secret motions of things; and the enlarging of the bounds of humane empire to the effecting of all things possible." [11] Indeed, Wells's famous exhortation for the application of science is no more than an expansion of Bacon's statement:

The plain message physical science has for the world at large is this, that were our political and social and moral devices only as well contrived to their ends as a linotype machine, an antiseptic operating plant, or an electric tram-car, there need now at the present moment be no appreciable toil in the world, and only the smallest fraction of the pain, the fear, and the anxiety that now makes human life so doubtful in its value. There is more than enough for everyone alive. Science stands, a too competent servant, behind her wrangling underbred masters, holding out resources, devices, and remedies they are too stupid to use. And on its material side a modern Utopia must needs present these gifts as taken, and show a world that is really abolishing the need of labour, abolishing the last base reason for anyone's servitude or inferiority. (*MU* 102)

Accordingly it is not surprising that A *Modern Utopia* is filled with machines and pervaded by Wells's manifest liking for them, a quality particularly offensive to most of the writers of anti-utopias in the twentieth century. Wells frankly could not see anything inherently ugly or evil about the machine:

There is nothing in machinery, there is nothing in embankments and railways and iron bridges and engineering devices to oblige them to be ugly. Ugliness is the measure of imperfection; a thing of human making is for the most part ugly in proportion to the poverty of its constructive thought, to the failure of its producer fully to grasp the purpose of its being. (*MU* 110)

But whatever men give continual thought and attention to, whatever they make and remake in order to do as well as they can, "grows beautiful inevitably." And so it is with machines; everything we do under modern conditions is ugly because our way of life is ugly, "because we live in an atmosphere of snatch and uncertainty, and do everything in an underbred and strenuous manner," which is the "misfortune of machinery and not its fault" (p. 111).

A fourth distinctive feature of A *Modern Utopia*—and another major contribution to utopian thought—is the idea that utopia is not static perfection but an ever evolving dynamism. One can, says Wells, no longer construct the kind of "Nowheres and Utopias men planned before Darwin quickened the thought of the world":

Those were all perfect and static States, a balance of happiness won for ever against the forces of unrest and disorder that inhere in things. One beheld a healthy and simple generation enjoying the fruits of the earth in an atmosphere of virtue and happiness, to be followed by other virtuous, happy, and entirely similar generations, until the Gods grew weary. Change and development were dammed back by invincible dams for ever. (*MU* 5)

Such a conception is no longer possible, and the modern utopia must be kinetic, not static, must shape itself "not as a permanent state but as a hopeful stage, leading to a long ascent of stages." (As we will see, an important later stage is described in *Men Like Gods.*)

These four distinctive and major features—Utopia as a World State; the voluntary nobility, the *samurai*; the important role of science and technology; and Utopia seen as kinetic, not static—determine the particular coloring of most of the subsidiary details of marriage, family, education, employment, and so forth, details which in many instances are at the same time recognizable modifications of elements of earlier utopias. Wells, of course, deals with all the familiar categories of life in Utopia.

The Utopian World State is a vast organization, a global bureaucracy. It is the "sole landowner of the earth," and holding feudally under it as landlords are the great local governments, which administer large areas of the world. The World State, often through its subordinate local governments, "holds all the sources of energy, and either directly or through its tenants, farmers and agents, develops these sources, and renders the energy available for the work of life":

It or its tenants will produce food, and so human energy, and the exploitation of coal and electric power, and the powers of wind and wave and water will be within its right. It will pour out this energy by assignment and lease and acquiescence and what not upon its individual citizens. (*MU* 89)

Naturally the World State maintains order, roads, and a cheap and efficient administration of justice; naturally it provides cheap and rapid locomotion and is the common carrier of the planet.

Under the protection of the great state, a limited form of capitalism survives, though wealth accumulated through buying and selling is not easily passed on to one's descendants. There is, of course, unqualified private property in those things that become extensions and expressions of a man's personality: "his clothing, his jewels, the tools of his employment, his books, the objects of art he may have bought or made, his personal weapons (if Utopia have need of such things), insignia, and so forth" (p. 92). But there is no private property in land or natural objects or products.

The Utopian World State is, as I have noted, an archetypal welfare state, and it is significant that *A Modern Utopia* was published just at the beginning of the Liberal government's eight-year reign, during which England moved well along toward being one of the most advanced of the "socialistically paternal" states of the twentieth century. In any case Wells's World State makes sure that every citizen is "properly housed, well nourished, and in good health, reasonably clean and clothed healthily." If he is unemployed where he lives, it helps him to find work in another area or finds him publicly supported work. It nurses and houses those who are sick, incapacitated, or old, and relief is supported by a kind of social security tax. But nowhere does the state exhibit a more benevolent interest in its citizens than in the area of family and population control.

The principle governing the state's interference in this area is that when a child is conceived, the future of the species is involved, and the state must represent this larger interest. There is no state breeding, as in Plato, since Wells realized how complex human heredity is; but the state regulates parenthood with certain requirements designed to insure that the "man who is 'poor' all around" is in the descendent—"the rather spiritless, rather incompetent low-grade man who on earth sits in the den of the sweater [sweatshop], tramps the streets under the banner of the unemployed, or trembles—in another man's cast-off clothing, and with an infinity of hat-touching—on the verge of rural employment" (p. 136). The requirements for parenthood attempt to make sure that a man has achieved a certain standard of personal efficiency by requiring him to earn at least a minimum wage and be free of debt, to have attained at least a minimum of physical development, to be free of any transmissible disease, and not to be a criminal. (Drunkards, criminals, and other social misfits are exiled to prison islands, where they are prevented from reproducing themselves.) To encourage proper nurture of the children in the family, motherhood is regarded as a service to the state, with regular payments for each child and increased money for superior children.

The perfect symbol of the persistent interest which the Utopian World State takes in its citizens is the great central index to all the world's inhabitants, which is housed in Paris. Every human being is classified there by such inalterable physical traits as fingerprints, and a record is kept on a card of pertinent material facts, such as marriage, criminal convictions, and so forth. Thus it is always possible for the state to identify any person quickly, while it is kept informed of each individual's location at any time. This system of identification is necessary because the population of Utopia is incredibly migratory, endlessly coming and going, "a people as fluid and tidal as the sea":

Now the simple laws of custom, the homely methods of identification that served in the little communities of the past when everyone knew everyone, fail in the face of this liquefaction [of the social body]. If the modern Utopia is indeed to be a world of responsible citizens, it must have devised some scheme by which every person in the world can be promptly and certainly recognised, and by which anyone missing can be traced and found. (*MU* 162)

All this "organized clairvoyance" would, of course, as Wells admitted, profoundly disturb the eighteenth- and nineteenth-century Liberal, "brought up to be against the Government on principle." But such a reaction, says Wells, represents only "mental habits acquired in an evil time":

The old Liberalism assumed bad government, the more powerful the government the worse it was, just as it assumed the natural righteousness of the free individual. Darkness and secrecy were, indeed, the natural refuges of liberty when every government had in it the near possibility of tyranny, and the Englishman or American looked at the papers of a Russian or a German as one might look at the chains of a slave. (*MU* 165)

But in a modern utopia the government is not bad, while the individual cannot always be counted on to be good—and so Wells attempted to meet the argument against there being such an all-seeing eye of the state. What Wells demanded in all his planning of Utopia is that the worst of human egotisms will be swept away:

If we are to have any Utopia at all, we must have a clear common purpose, and a great and steadfast movement of will to override all these incurably egotistical dissentients. Something is needed wide and deep enough to float the worst of egotisms away. The world is not to be made right by acclamation and in a day, and then for ever more trusted to run alone. It is manifest this Utopia could not come about by chance and anarchy, but by co-ordinated effort and a community of design. . . . (*MU* 128)

(It has been easy for critics to seize upon this and other statements as proof that Wells cared little for human freedom in *A Modern Utopia*, but to do so is to ignore his carefully reasoned argument early in the book that the state must provide each individual with the maximum liberty consistent with that of others.)

But besides the economic, social, and political arrangements, the spirit of a modern utopia is conveyed by a few well-chosen details of the way people live, how they dress, what they look like, how they travel. The sense of order and purpose lying behind this great World State is nowhere made more vivid than in the architecture of Utopian London, an astonishing sight to the narrator, who comes from early Edwardian London.

It is a city designed by the artist-engineer, who builds, with thought and steel, structures lighter than stone or brick can yield, having completely discarded the past, having discarded "the squat temple boxes of the Greek, the buxom curvatures of Rome." With its towering buildings, its moving ways, its domes of glass and great arches, it is distantly akin to the London of *When the Sleeper Wakes* and "A Story of the Days To Come," as well as a forecast of the modern architecture which ultimately traces its origins to the Crystal Palace of 1851 (a building Wells would have seen in its new form and location at South Kensington):

They will have flung great arches and domes of glass above the wider spaces of the town, the slender beauty of the perfect metal-work far overhead will be softened to a fairy-like unsubstantiality by the mild London air. . . . The gay and swiftly moving platforms of the public ways will go past on either hand, carrying sporadic groups of people, and very speedily we shall find ourselves in a sort of central space, rich with palms and flowering bushes and statuary. We shall look along an avenue of trees, down a wide gorge between the cliffs of crowded hotels, the hotels that are still glowing with internal lights, to where the shining morning river streams dawnlit out to sea. (*MU* 244)

In these hotels or in private clubs most of the people live, for the autonomy of the private household has been greatly reduced.

The same sense of mind at work, with its resultant functionalism, is apparent in other details of life Wells chooses to give us. Thus we see it in the simple austere dress of the Utopians, in the description of the room in the inn in which the visitors stay, in the description of the 200-mile-an-hour train in which they travel from Lucerne to London. It is also apparent in the good looks and the healthy bodies of the Utopians themselves: "Everyone is well grown and well nourished; everyone seems in good condition; everyone walks well, and has that clearness of eye that comes with clearness of blood" (p. 314). And wrinkled old age is forestalled by a sounder physiological science than ours:

They have put off the years of decay. They keep their teeth, they keep their digestions, they ward off gout and rheumatism, neuralgia and influenza and all those cognate decays that bend and wrinkle men and women in the middle years of existence. They have extended the level years far into the seventies, and age, when it comes, comes swiftly and easily. The feverish hurry of our earth, the decay that begins before growth has ceased, is replaced by a ripe prolonged maturity. (*MU* 315)

This prolonged maturity followed swiftly by the end becomes, of course, an important detail in *Brave New World.*

And then suddenly from this beautiful world, when the narrator's vision of it is most complete, we are thrown back to London:

There is no jerk, no sound, no hint of material shock. We are in London, and clothed in the fashion of the town. The sullen roar of London fills our ears. . . . (*MU* 358)

Everywhere there is disorder, noise, crowding, filth:

What a lot of filthy, torn paper is scattered about the world! We walk slowly side by side towards the dirt-littered basin of the fountain, and stand regarding two grimy tramps who sit and argue on a further seat. One holds a horrible old boot in his hand, and gesticulates with it, while his other hand caresses his rag-wrapped foot. (*MU* 60)

Then the narrator and his companion walk on past men and women and children struggling about a string of omnibuses, then pause to look at a newly spread newspaper placard (reminiscent of the newspaper in Bellamy's *Looking Backward* which Julian West sees when he dreams that he is back in the nineteenth century):

Massacre in Odessa

Discovery of Human Remains at Chertsey

SHOCKING LYNCHING OUTRAGE IN NEW YORK STATE

German Intrigues Get a Set-Back

The Birthday Honours—Full List

"Dear old familiar world!" comments the narrator (p. 360). And so by a series of similar contrasts Wells underlines the sweet sanity of an ordered world utopia.

III

The second stage in the evolution of utopia is presented in *Men Like Gods* (1923)—a book generally well written and well conceived, though in intellectual vigor somewhat inferior to *A Modern Utopia*. It starts off with something of the careful domestication of the impossible which we have seen characterizes the best of Wells's scientific romances, the gaining of credibility so essential to successful fiction about other worlds, marvelous inventions, or any of the other themes of science fiction. Mr. Barnstaple, a liberal journalist, drives off on vacation to escape from his boisterous family and, most of all, from the conflict and unreason in human affairs:

The great coal lock-out had been going on for a month and seemed to foreshadow the commercial ruin of England; every morning brought intelligence of fresh outrages from Ireland, unforgivable and unforgettable outrages; a prolonged drought threatened the harvests of the world; the League of Nations, of which Mr. Barnstaple had hoped enormous things in the great days of President Wilson, was a melancholy and self-satisfied futility; everywhere there was conflict, everywhere unreason; seven-eighths of the world seemed to be sinking down towards chronic disorder and social dissolution. (MLG 3)

A little way out of Slough he is passed by a touring car and a limousine, only to discover that the road ahead is perfectly clear, without a trace of the vehicles which have passed him. And then before he knows what is happening, his car seems to strike something and skids:

Afterwards he remembered that at this point he heard a sound. It was exactly the same sound, coming as the climax of an accumulating pressure, sharp like the snapping of a lute string, which one hears at the end—or beginning—of insensibility under anaesthetic. (MLG 12)

He stops in profoundest astonishment to discover that he is on an entirely different road from the one he had been upon half a minute before. The hedges and trees have changed, and instead of Windsor Castle there are snow-clad mountains in the distance. What has happened is that Mr. Barnstaple and the people in the other two cars have been translated to Utopia, a world lying in a parallel universe, translated as the result of experiments with the F Dimension being conducted in that other world.

As he learns about the new world, Mr. Barnstaple becomes increasingly enthusiastic, but the rest of the Earth-lings soon despise its order and beauty, preferring earthly muddle and ugliness. The book is thus a satire on the people whom Wells saw as the enemies of the scientific reorganization of society, including at least two characters recognizable as Wells's contemporaries—Lord Balfour and Winston Churchill. The most biting of these portraits is that of Churchill as Rupert Catskill, who organizes and leads an unsuccessful attempt on the part of the little group of Earth-lings to seize power from the Utopians and make another earth out of the new world. Catskill dreams of empire, and Barnstaple denounces him roundly:

"You have a very good imagination," Mr. Barnstaple reflected. "The trouble is that you have been so damnably educated. What is the trouble with you? You are be-Kiplinged. Empire and Anglo-Saxon and boy-scout and sleuth are the stuff in your mind. If I had gone to Eton I might have been the same as you are, I suppose."

"Harrow," corrected Mr. Catskill. (MLG 179)

Wells gives Catskill the dubious honor of being the most articulate enemy of the order and beauty of Utopia and has him stating the standard conservative arguments against the desirability of a utopia. The crux of Mr. Catskill's position is the necessity for pain and hardship and difficulty. First of all, he argues, these things are necessary to throw into contrast the bright moments of life, are necessary for our happiness:

"The rats gnaw and the summer flies persecute and madden. At times life reeks and stinks. I admit it, Sir, I admit it. We go down far below your extremest experiences into discomforts and miseries, anxieties and anguish of soul and body, into bitterness, terror and despair. Yea. But do we not also go higher? I challenge you with that. What can you know in this immense safety of the intensity, the frantic, terror-driven intensity, of many of our efforts? What can you know of reprieves and interludes and escapes? Think of our happinesses beyond your ken!" (MLG 82)

Second, Catskill argues, struggle and competition and conflict themselves evolve energy and beauty; without them men would degenerate.

Urthred, the spokesman for Utopia, answers that there is no way but knowledge out of the cages of life. His position is what we have seen Wells learned from Huxley. If we allowed unhampered competition and struggle for survival, then we allow nature to rule:

> "These Earthlings do not yet dare to see what our Mother Nature is. At the back of their minds is still the desire to abandon themselves to her. They do not see that except for our eyes and wills, she is purposeless and blind. She is not awful, she is horrible. She takes no heed to our standards, nor to any standards of excellence. She made us by accident; all her children are bastards—undesired; she will cherish or expose them, pet or starve or torment without rhyme or reason. She does not heed, she does not care. She will lift us up to power and intelligence, or debase us to the mean feebleness of the rabbit or the slimy white filthiness of a thousand of her parasitic inventions. There must be good in her because she made all that is good in us—but also there is endless evil. Do not your Earthlings see the dirt of her, the cruelty, the insane indignity of much of her work?" (MLG 87)

But for us the greatest significance of *Men Like Gods* is that it presents a utopia in a later stage of evolution than does *A Modern Utopia*, a fact Wells himself admitted in the preface to the book as republished in the Atlantic Edition. And it is also 3000 years ahead of our earth, where we are still in what the Utopians call the Age of Confusion.

Perhaps the most noticeable way in which the Utopia of *Men Like Gods* differs from that of *A Modern Utopia*, which was only a little ahead of us, is that all government has withered away. Instead of judges and legislators and rulers, there are only experts doing their jobs scientifically and rationally. Instead of our confusions and conflict, there are only people living together in order and peace because they have been educated to do so:

> Utopia has no parliament, no politics, no private wealth, no business competition, no police nor prisons, no lunatics, no defectives nor cripples, and it has none of these things because it has schools and teachers who are all that schools and teachers can be. Politics, trade and competition are the methods of adjustment of a crude society. Such methods of adjustment have been laid aside in Utopia for more than a thousand years. There is no rule nor government needed by adult Utopians because all the rule and government they need they have had in childhood and youth. (*MLG* 64)

As one of them explains, "Our education is our government" (p. 65).

A corollary of this withering away of government in *Men Like Gods* is the fact that, by means of the eugenic control begun in *A Modern Utopia* and by means of the unique emphasis on education, inferior individuals no longer exist and the ruling class of the *samurai* has been extended to include everyone. It is really a world of people who are superior to us—healthier, stronger, more intelligent, more self-disciplined.

Indeed, *Men Like Gods* differs from *A Modern Utopia* in being much more a dream vision, much less a detailed blueprint. In part it is a kind of hymn to a world incredibly more lovely, orderly, healthy, energetic:

Nearly all the greater evils of human life had been conquered; war, pestilence and malaise, famine and poverty had been swept out of human experience. The dreams of artists, of perfected and lovely bodies and of a world transfigured to harmony and beauty had been realized; the spirits of order and organization ruled triumphant. Every aspect of human life had been changed by these achievements. (*MLG* 211)

And what Mr. Barnstaple sees is only "a beginning, no more than a beginning":

"Some day here and everywhere, Life of which you and I are but anticipatory atoms and eddies, Life will awaken indeed, one and whole and marvelous, like a child awaking to conscious life. It will open its drowsy eyes and stretch itself and smile, looking the mystery of God in the face as one meets the morning sun. We shall be there then, all that matters of us, you and I. . . ." (*MLG* 248)

But while *Men Like Gods* differs from *A Modern Utopia*, the same utopian imagination is still at work. Thus there is the same faith in science and hope for material progress, the same willingness to accept the machine. And there are also various details hardly changed from *A Modern Utopia*, such as the prolongation of youth; the great central index to the world's inhabitants; a population incredibly migratory; the cleaning up of the planet and extermination of tiresome and mischievous species, from animals to micro-organisms; even cremation instead of burial.

CHAPTER V

W

ITH E. M. FORSTER's "The Machine Stops" [1] (1909),
we have the first full-scale emergence of the twentieth-
century anti-utopia. "The Machine Stops" begins the
series of "admonitory satires" that includes Zamyatin's
We, Huxley's *Brave New World,* and Orwell's *Nineteen
Eighty-four.* In portraying mechanical superstates which take
away human freedom, isolate men from nature, and destroy
the past, these anti-utopias are appallingly similar, first of all
because they are Wellsian science fiction rich in anti-utopian
images originated by Wells. They also represent massive
attacks on the Wellsian vision of utopia we described in
Chapter IV.

The anti-utopias show many similarities in their reactions

to Wells, because there was much interaction and influence among these works themselves. *We,* for example, influenced *Nineteen Eighty-four,* as Orwell's article, "Freedom and Happiness," [2] clearly proves. Furthermore, although Huxley claimed never to have read *We,* he knew of it; while Orwell must have read "The Machine Stops," and there is a possibility that Zamyatin did also.

That the writers of major anti-utopias valued each other's work is not surprising, given the similarity of their points of view. Their attacks represent what George Woodcock has called "the criticism of Utopia . . . from the disillusioned left," [3] a criticism expressed in the familiar quotation from Nicholas Berdyaev with which Huxley prefaces *Brave New World:*

Utopias are realisable . . . and towards utopias we are moving. But it is possible that a new age is already beginning, in which cultured and intelligent people will dream of ways to avoid ideal states and to get back to a society that is less "perfect" and more free. [4]

The rejection of the idea of utopia and the toppling of Wells from his position as leader of a generation are part of a single phenomenon: the cultural shift, brought by the catastrophe of World War I, which tended to lead men to a disillusioned and austere traditionalism, to a return to the doctrine of original sin. This caused "progress" to become a bad word, a transformation which in its turn helped to alienate many who earlier had been attracted by the Wellsian vision. But one must also concede that contributing to the loss of respect for Wells's ideas was the evidence of Wells's "messianic delusion" and the resulting decline in his powers as artist. In any case, by the 1920's most intellectuals had turned against Wells. Their attitude was brilliantly captured in Mark Rampion's caricature of "The Outline of History according to Mr. H. G. Wells" in Huxley's *Point Counter Point:*

The drawing on the left was composed on the lines of a simple crescendo. A very small monkey was succeeded by a very slightly larger pithecanthropus, which was succeeded in its turn by a slightly larger Neanderthal man. Paleolithic man, neolithic man, bronze-age Egyptian and Babylonian man, iron-age Greek and Roman man—the figures slowly increased in size. By the time Galileo and Newton had appeared on the scene, humanity had grown to quite respectable dimensions. The crescendo continued uninterrupted through Watt and Stevenson, Faraday and Darwin, Bessemer and Edison, Rockefeller and Wanamaker to come to a contemporary consummation in the figures of Mr. H. G. Wells himself and Sir Alfred Mond. Nor was the future neglected. Through the radiant mist of prophecy the forms of Wells and Mond, growing larger and larger at every repetition, wound away in a triumphant spiral clean off the paper, toward Utopian infinity.[5]

Surely the nadir came in 1936 with the movie *Things to Come*. As Warren Wagar has pointed out, it was "Wells' worst, most lopsided Utopia, conceived in haste to hammer home one simple message to a mass audience incapable of digesting more than one idea at a time." [6] In the reviews one can find most of the stock objections to Wells expressed more vigorously than ever before or since. One of the most important of these is Michael Roberts's "Mr. Wells' Sombre World" in the *Spectator* for December 17, 1936. Roberts admitted that mechanical progress can benefit mankind, but he accused Wells of dangerously denying other important values and dimensions to life. His indictment is measured and sincere:

The fundamental objection to Mr. Wells's god of progress is that it is too limited; it takes no cognisance of the human soul or the human mind, but only of mathematical ability and manual skill. Its idea of greatness is merely one of size, not one of quality. A journey to the moon, and not something like the composition of Beethoven's A minor quartet, is treated as the greatest achievement possible to man.[7]

Communists, fascists, liberals, and Christians joined in denouncing Wells's seeming infatuation with mechanical progress as manifested in *Things to Come*. More than ever before, "Wellsian" had come to mean a glittering, padded world, filled with mechanical wonders and super-gadgets and run by an aristocracy of scientists and engineers and managers for the good of the mass of people. All of this distorted and misrepresented Wells's most cherished ideas. He was, after all, a kind of superhumanist, who dreamed of putting man on the throne of the universe, who believed that, by the use of reason, order and beauty could be brought to human life. But to a very great extent the anti-utopians, both before as well as after 1936, failed to see this.

The two earliest major anti-utopias, "The Machine Stops" (1909) and *We* (1924), together represent what might be considered the first wave of anti-utopian reaction in fiction. Of all the anti-utopias, they are probably the closest to Wells, which is doubtless why they are so surprisingly alike in the mechanical quality of the life they depict. Forster in his anti-utopianism is, of course, far in advance of his time.

II

There can be no question that "The Machine Stops" is a Wellsian scientific romance set in a Wellsian future, the only significant difference in technique being that Forster, like most later anti-utopians, does not take the trouble to domesticate the incredible as Wells does in his best romances. And so in "The Machine Stops" we start out, not in the here and now, but in a distant future, in this case a world where men live underground in hexagonal cells, tier on tier, almost their every need and desire satisfied through the agency of the Machine. Friends communicate by means of television phones without ever meeting; lectures and concerts are piped into the cells so that no one need go to a public gathering; even medical diagnosis and treatment can be given by automatic apparatus installed in each cell. Indeed, each cell is a pushbutton paradise, with conditioned air and artificial illumination. So adapted have men become to this unnatural existence that they spend almost their whole adult life in isolation in their cells, avoiding direct experience and living only in their imaginations. And in time men come to worship the Machine on which they are so dependent.

Hardly ever does anyone visit the surface of the earth, for it is supposed to be inhospitable to human life. "The surface of the earth," Vashti reminds her son Kuno, "is only dust and mud, no life remains on it, and you would need a respirator, or the cold of the outer air would kill you" (p. 6). Punishment for crime against civilization and the Machine is Homelessness—being forced out on the surface, which supposedly means death. At the end of the story, when the Machine has broken down and the people underground are dying, hopelessly unfit to save themselves, we are told that some men have survived outside and with them lies the future of humanity: "I have seen them, spoken to them, loved them. They are hiding in the mist and ferns until our civilisation stops" (p. 61).

Unquestionably "The Machine Stops" attacks the Wellsian vision. Forster, in the introduction to the 1947 edition of his stories, wrote, " 'The Machine Stops' is a counterblast to one of the heavens of H. G. Wells." But much the same thing had already been said by various critics. Thus Lionel Trilling in 1943 called the story "a counter-Wellsian fantasy of the future life," and G. Lowes Dickinson in 1928 praised Forster on the occasion of the publication of the story in *The Eternal Moment* for turning the "Wells-Shaw prophecies" inside out.[8]

Since "The Machine Stops" was first published only five years after *A Modern Utopia*, it seems likely that the latter was very much in Forster's mind. Certainly it is in spirit and detail an inversion of the future seen by Wells in *A Modern Utopia*. The controlling principle for this inversion is Forster's humanism.

"Forster's persistent 'moral,' " wrote Frederick Crews, "is that the life of affectionate personal relations, disengaged from political and religious zeal by means of a tolerant eclecticism, is supremely valuable." [9] Along with Forster's belief in the value of the "life of affectionate personal relations" goes a powerful respect for the individual, a respect which in its turn leads him to fear that the planners of the organized state will crush that individuality. The planners, he wrote,

assure us that the new economy will evolve an appropriate morality, and then when all people are properly fed and housed, they will have an outlook which will be right, because they are the people. I cannot swallow that. I have no mystic faith in the people. I have in the individual. He seems to me a divine achievement and I mistrust any view which belittles him. [10]

This faith in the individual is connected in an almost mystical way with the beauties of scenery and landscape. Crews explained this feature of Forster's humanism very well:

The landscapes in his novels have an almost pantheistic vitality, and they are usually enlisted on the side of self-realization for the central characters. To be attuned to the spirit of the countryside is not simply to resist the shallowness of London, but to be awake to the full life of the senses, without which there is no real awakening of the soul. [11]

Finally, Crews showed how Forster believed that the free and civilized human spirit will achieve its fullest self-fulfillment through art:

In purging itself of moral inconsistencies, one segment of nineteenth-century liberalism broke free from the greatest-happiness principle and seized upon an ideal of individual self-cultivation that could find complete embodiment only in art—and Forster's art will prove to be both sustained and, in the last analysis, restricted by that ideal.[12]

It is from the point of view of these articles of humanist faith that Forster attacked the Wellsian utopia.

Forster's starting point was the World State itself. "The Machine Stops" presents a logical development from the regimented, planned World State of A Modern Utopia, including even its eugenic control. Wells described this World State with love, and by his gifts of expression he makes us feel that it is something good and fine, a state where human happiness might have a better chance of being achieved than in any state that has ever existed before. Forster took the same state and showed how it could come to stifle the individual, crush human ingenuity and inventiveness, destroy art, and enfeeble men—in fact, turn them into machines.

But while Forster was concerned with the effects on the individual of the kind of planned state Wells dreamed of, he was much more concerned—and really spent most of his time attacking—Wells's faith in and enthusiasm for the machine and the importance Wells seemed to assign to the machine in his utopian vision.

A Modern Utopia, to a sensitive artist like Forster, reeks offensively of the machine. For example, consider the attitude toward the machine implicit in Well's discussion of utopian transportation. A young Edison would no doubt welcome the spirit of the passage, but how different would be the reaction of the English literary intellectual:

No doubt the Utopian will travel in many ways. It is unlikely there will be any smoke-disgorging steam trains in Utopia, they are already doomed on earth, already threatened with that obsolescence that will endear them to the Ruskins of to-morrow, but a thin spider's web of inconspicuous special routes will cover the land of the world, pierce the mountain masses and tunnel under the seas. These may be double railways or monorails or what not—we are not engineers to judge between such devices—but by means of them the Utopian will travel about the earth from one chief point to another at a speed of two or three hundred miles an hour. That will abolish the greater distances. . . . (*MU* 45)

The snide reference to Ruskin would not, I think, exactly help Wells in proving the value of the machine to Forster, nor would Wells's portrayal of the opponent of mechanization and the advocate of a return to nature in *A Modern Utopia* "as a *poseur* beyond question, a conscious Ishmaelite in the world of wit, and in some subtly inexplicable way as a most consummate ass" (p. 116). This spokesman for the opposition—affected in dress, manner, and speech—is almost a caricature of a literary intellectual.

Even when Wells steps in to argue persuasively for the importance of science and technology in Utopia, it seems very unlikely that he will win any converts among the literary intellectuals. Thus we have the passage, quoted in Chapter IV, which begins:

The plain message physical science has for the world at large is this, that were our political and social and moral devices only as well contrived to their ends as a linotype machine, an antiseptic operating plant, or an electric tram-car, there need now at the present moment be no appreciable toil in the world, and only the smallest fraction of the pain, the fear, and the anxiety that now makes human life so doubtful in its value. (*MU* 102)

Forster in "The Machine Stops" gives expression to some of the most important humanist fears about the machine— the fear that the machine will lead to the mechanization of human life and finally to the control of human life; the fear that the machine will dwarf men and take from them their self-respect, pride, and sense of uniqueness; the fear that reliance on the machine will be not only psychologically and spiritually harmful but in the end physically destructive; and the fear that men may even come to make of the machine a false idol which they will worship. "Man is the measure," says Kuno, Forster's spokesman in the story:

"Near" is a place to which I can get quickly *on my feet*, not a place to which the train or air-ship will take me quickly. "Far" is a place to which I cannot get quickly on my feet; the vomitory is "far," though I could be there in thirty-eight seconds by summoning the train. Man is the measure. That was my first lesson. Man's feet are the measure for distance, his hands are the measure for ownership, his body is the measure for all that is lovable and desirable and strong. (*MS* 27)

In *A Modern Utopia*, as Forster reads it, Wells has made the machine the measure.

At this point it is relevant to note that Forster's hatred of the machine owes something to Samuel Butler.[13] Forster's anxieties about the machine are more or less congruent with those of the Erewhonians who, long before the narrator traveled over the range, destroyed most of the machines because they feared that the machines would evolve intelligence and will and, being more efficient than man, come to replace him. The arguments advanced against the machine in the Erewhonian "Book of the Machine" (note, too, that Forster uses this title for the book that gives all the necessary instructions on how to operate the Machine) are echoed in this statement by Kuno:

Cannot you see, cannot all your lecturers see, that it is we who are dying, and that down here the only thing that really lives is the Machine? We created the Machine, to do our will, but we cannot make it do our will now. It has robbed us of the sense of space and of the sense of touch, it has blurred every human relation and narrowed down love to a carnal act; it has paralyzed our bodies and our wills, and now it compels us to worship it. The Machine develops—but not on our lines. The Machine proceeds—but not to our goal. We only exist as the blood corpuscles that course through its arteries, and if it could work without us, it would let us die. (*MS* 37)

Forster, there can be no doubt, is an Erewhonian machine-breaker.

Ironically, it is science fiction as developed by Wells that Forster uses as the vehicle for his polemic against the machine. Most of the imaginative vitality of "The Machine Stops" derives from Wells—from *A Modern Utopia*, of course, but also from several of the great scientific romances.

But, to return to *A Modern Utopia*, Forster's borrowings from it are both important and rather obvious. For example, the windowless train of Utopia becomes, as A. L. Morton has noted, the utter lack of desire on the part of the people of Forster's world to look out of the window of the automatic aircraft.[14] Forster develops this idea at some length when, through Vashti's reaction to the great monuments on the surface of the earth, he makes a none-too-subtle point about the people of the Machine. Vashti, reluctantly flying to her son in the Southern Hemisphere, glances from time to time out of the windows of the aircraft:

At midday she took a second glance at the earth. The air-ship was crossing another range of mountains, but she could see little, owing to the clouds. Masses of black rock hovered below her, and merged indistinctly into grey. Their shapes were fantastic; one of them resembled a prostrate man.

"No ideas here," murmured Vashti, and hid the Caucasus behind a metal blind.

In the evening she looked again. They were crossing a golden sea, in which lay many small islands and one peninsula.

She repeated, "No ideas here," and hid Greece behind a metal blind. (*MS* 23)

Another important group of details comes from the description of living arrangements in *A Modern Utopia*—Wells sees most people living in apartments and eating their meals in communal dining halls. His description of one such apartment is very evidently the inspiration for the cell rooms in which the underground people in Forster's world live:

It is beautifully proportioned, and rather lower than most rooms I know on earth. There is no fireplace, and I am perplexed by that until I find a thermometer beside six switches on the wall. Above this switch-board is a brief instruction: one switch warms the floor, which is not carpeted, but covered by a substance like soft oilcloth; one warms the mattress (which is of metal with resistance coils threaded to and fro in it); and the others warm the wall in various degrees, each directing current through a separate system of resistances. The casement does not open, but above, flush with the ceiling, a noiseless rapid fan pumps air out of the room. (*MU* 103–4)

Completing the arrangements is a bed which folds up into the wall. From pushbuttons to ventilation to the receding bed, this apartment is obviously the prototype of the cells in "The Machine Stops." Forster takes Wells to the ultimate absurdity, as in the opening paragraph:

Imagine, if you can, a small room, hexagonal in shape, like the cell of a bee. It is lighted neither by window nor lamp, yet it is filled with a soft radiance. There are no apertures for ventilation, yet the air is fresh. There are no musical instruments, and yet, at the moment my meditation opens, this room is throbbing with melodious sounds. An arm-chair is in the centre, by its side a reading-desk—that is all the furniture. (*MS* 1)

Needless to say, the chair is worked by machinery.

But Forster does something more important than take details from Wells: he exaggerates and parodies the spirit of Wells's Utopia, making Wells seem to recommend the reduction of life to a barren, mechanical simplicity. Thus Forster's comment on the loss which came in using the Machine to communicate:

. . . the Machine did not transmit *nuances* of expression. It only gave a general idea of people—an idea that was good enough for all practical purposes, Vashti thought. The imponderable bloom, declared by a discredited philosophy to be the actual essence of intercourse, was rightly ignored by the Machine, just as the imponderable bloom of the grape was ignored by the manufacturers of artificial fruit. Something "good enough" had long since been accepted by our race. (*MS* 5)

Indeed, many of Forster's values are antithetical to those of Wells's, such as, for example, the life of affectionate personal relationships. Vashti, and presumably all the other adults in the world of the Machine, sin against this value not only by living in isolation from each other but by allowing their children to be raised by the state in public nurseries and thereby never feeling any strong love and attachment for them—we need only remember here the role of public crèches in Wells's *When the Sleeper Wakes* and "A Story of the Days To Come."

Nature is another element in Forster's humanistic world opposed to Wells's values. Thus Kuno's animistic description of what he sees as he peeks over the "grass-grown hollow that was edged with fern"—a line of "low colourless hills":

But to me they were living and the turf that covered them was a skin, under which their muscles rippled, and I felt that those hills had called with incalculable force to men in the past, and that men had loved them. Now they sleep—perhaps for ever. They commune with humanity in dreams. Happy the man, happy the woman, who awakes the hills of Wessex. For though they sleep, they will never die. (*MS* 36)

Indeed, Forster has read *A Modern Utopia* very well. He has also, as we have noted, taken various details from Wells's five great scientific romances. The great beehive of underground cells, for example, is the world inside the moon in *The First Men in the Moon*. But more important are Forster's debts to *The Time Machine*. The ventilation shaft through which Kuno crawls to the outside is the same shaft down which the Time Traveler climbs for his hasty and nearly fatal look at the subterranean Morlocks. Further, the people underground in "The Machine Stops" are evolving in the direction predicted by Wells in the form of the Elois: physical strength, energy and self-reliance have been weeded out as degeneration and decay follow luxury and ease.

Recently Wilfred Stone has implied that *The Time Machine* is the particular heaven which Forster was attacking in "The Machine Stops." [15] But this can hardly be the full explanation, even if Forster himself should now offer it, since "The Machine Stops" is so very obviously an attack on the Wellsian vision of a utopian World State, at the same time that *The Time Machine* is so very obviously an anti-utopia. It would be more accurate to say that "The Machine Stops" is an imitation of *The Time Machine*, for both are basically the same story: science fiction warning us of a distant future after science and technology have triumphed and men, as a result, have deteriorated. And Wells's is the better story of the two.

Finally we should note that in "The Machine Stops," whose chief purpose is to attack the machine, are embedded political and social elements much more prominent in later anti-utopias, some of which elements we have seen making their first appearance in other Wellsian scientific romances, most notably in *When the Sleeper Wakes*, "A Story of the Days To Come," and *The First Men in the Moon*. Thus Homelessness, the punishment for crime against the Machine, looks forward to the vaporizations and other executions so often employed against enemies of the state in subsequent anti-utopias, while the Central Committee, which supervises everyone and everything, foreshadows Big Brothers, Well-Doers, and World Controllers. Indeed, the underground world is essentially the regimented state of the anti-utopias, though this is not emphasized. Then there are other familiar anti-utopian elements: we learn, for example, of a Great Rebellion which took place long before the time of the story, and we also see history being falsified by a long succession of lecturers who warn their listeners to beware of firsthand ideas. And in addition to the eugenic control we have already noted, the state also practices euthanasia.

A work which must be discussed here, since it is frequently associated with Forster's story, is Karel Čapek's play, R.U.R. In 1921 it introduced the symbol of the robot to the world (the term had previously been coined by Joseph Čapek), and it is usually regarded as the almost archetypal expression of the fear that men will be enslaved and dehumanized by their own machines. It is not, however, at all a developed anti-utopia, even to the extent of "The Machine Stops," although it is obviously a Wellsian scientific romance, partly anti-utopian in spirit. Echoing Mary Shelley's *Frankenstein* as well as the Jewish legend of the Golem of Prague,[16] R.U.R. is the story of how, on a "distant island," the firm of Rossum's Universal Robots manufactures millions of artificial men to do the world's work. This industry had its start many years earlier, when old Rossum, the scientist, had set about perfecting a method for artificially creating life so that he could prove belief in God unnecessary. Young Rossum, his engineer son, then took over the process and put it on an efficient mass-produced basis, founding the firm of Rossum's. The play deals chiefly with how the robots come to develop souls and eventually revolt and destroy their masters, but not before the secret of their manufacture is lost. In the Epilogue, the threatened cessation of consciousness is averted when two robots, Primus and Helena, fall in love and go forth, presumably the Adam and Eve of a new world.

It is important to emphasize that the play, whose chief symbol of the robot also owes something to earlier expressionist drama, particularly to George Kaiser's *Gas, Part I*, represents more than men enslaved by their machines. For Čapek, the meaning of the play was much more complex, as he explained in a rebuttal to interpretations constructed by Shaw, Chesterton, and Commander Kenworthy. "I wished to write," said Čapek, "a comedy, partly of science, partly of truth."

As Čapek explained it, the comedy of science more or less coincides with the familiar interpretation of the play as being about the tyranny of a scientific and mechanical civilization:

The old inventor, Mr. Rossum (whose name in English signifies Mr. Intellect or Mr. Brain), is no more or less than a typical representative of the scientific materialism of the last century. His desire to create an artificial man—in the chemical and biological, not the mechanical sense—is inspired by a foolish and obstinate wish to prove God to be unnecessary and absurd. Young Rossum is the modern scientist, untroubled by metaphysical ideas; scientific experiment is to him the road to industrial production, he is not concerned to prove, but to manufacture. To create a Homunculus is a medieval idea; to bring it in line with the present century this creation must be undertaken on the principle of mass-production. Immediately we are in the grip of industrialism; this terrible machinery must not stop, for if it does it would destroy the lives of thousands. It must, on the contrary, go on faster and faster, although it destroy in the process thousands and thousands of other existences. Those who think to master the industry are themselves mastered by it: Robots must be produced although they are, or rather *because* they are, a war industry. The conception of the human brain has at last escaped from the control of human nature. This is the comedy of science.

It is the comedy of truth which represents Čapek's other intentions:

Now for my other idea, the comedy of truth. The General Manager Domin, in the play, proves that technical progress emancipates man from hard manual labour, and he is quite right. The Tolstoyan Alquist, on the contrary, believes that technical progress demoralizes him, and I think he is right, too. Bussman thinks that industrialism alone is capable of supplying modern needs; he is right. Finally, the Robots themselves revolt against all these idealists, and, as it appears, they are right, too.[17]

The multiplicity of points of view is underscored when Domin, the factory manager, is allowed to make a strong defense of technological utopia:

DOMIN. I wanted man to become the master, so that he shouldn't live merely for a crust of bread. I wanted not a single soul to be broken by other people's machinery. I wanted nothing, nothing to be left of this appalling social structure. I'm revolted by poverty. I wanted a new generation. I wanted—I thought—

ALQUIST. Well?

DOMIN. I wanted to turn the whole of mankind into an aristocracy of the world. An aristocracy nourished by milliards of mechanical slaves. Unrestricted, free, and consummated in man. And maybe more than man.

ALQUIST. Superman?

DOMIN. Yes. Oh, only to have a hundred years of time! Another hundred years for the future of mankind. (R.U.R. 42)

Domin is Wells, and his dream of man on the throne of the universe is Wellsian. Čapek did not have Forster's hatred for Wells's ideas; in fact, he admired Wells and sought him out when he came to England in 1921, and in *Letters From England* he refers to Wells as "one of the wisest men." [18] This is why, though R.U.R. is partly an attack on the Wellsian vision, it is not thoroughly anti-Wellsianism. Its failure to be consistently anti-Wellsian is why R.U.R. does not portray a monstrous mechanical superstate regimenting humanity, why, in other words, it is not really an anti-utopia in the manner of *We* or even "The Machine Stops."

But, as we have noted, Čapek takes the form itself, the scientific romance, from Wells. And not only the form; Čapek also borrows details. As William Harkins has pointed out in *Karel Čapek*, certain details of old Rossum's experiments, as well as the island setting itself, may well have come from Wells's *The Island of Dr. Moreau*.[19] The following passage, for example, was surely written by someone familiar with *Moreau:*

It was in the year 1920 that old Rossum, the great physiologist, who was then quite a young scientist, took himself to this distant island for the purpose of studying the ocean fauna. . . . On this occasion he attempted by chemical synthesis to imitate the living matter known as protoplasm until he suddenly discovered a substance which behaved like living matter although its chemical composition was different. (*R.U.R.* 6)

And so old Rossum sets about imitating nature, first attempting an artificial dog. It would seem likely that *The Island of Dr. Moreau* and the legend of the Golem swirled around in Čapek's "deep well of unconscious cerebration" to finally be precipitated out in a new combination as *R.U.R.*

It is also possible that, as Harkins has suggested, there is an allusion to Wells's *The Food of the Gods* in the play:

DOMIN. He began to manufacture Super-Robots. Regular giants they were. He tried to make them twelve feet tall. But you wouldn't believe what a failure they were.

HELENA. A failure?

DOMIN. Yes. For no reason at all their limbs used to keep snapping off. Evidently our planet is too small for giants. Now we make only Robots of normal size and of a very high-class human finish. (*R.U.R.* 10)

Čapek, of course, went on to write other works which, though in part Wellsian scientific romances, are not anti-utopias. In *The Factory for the Absolute* (1922)—"a Wellsian idea treated in a Chestertonian manner" [20]—the destruction of matter to produce atomic energy brings also release of the Absolute which inheres in matter, a process leading to religious fanaticism, economic collapse, and a disastrous world war in which only thirteen men survive out of armies totaling 198,000,000. The novel is thus a kind of post-catastrophe story and as such is related to the anti-utopias. But the other works are completely unlike the anti-utopias with which we are dealing in this book. In *The Makropulos Secret* (1922), an unintentional answer to

Shaw's *Back to Methuselah,* eternal life is a curse and its secret is finally destroyed by youth. In *Krakatit* (1924), knowledge of the secret of atomic energy leads the engineer Prokop at last to a confrontation with God and a rededication of his talents to the service of humanity. Finally, in the brilliantly satiric *The War with the Newts,* the exploited newts, who are an expansion of the robot symbol, rise up against the world. The book simultaneously attacks capitalism, fascism, and communism, but again, like R.U.R., it does not really employ the image of the monstrous mechanical superstate, although it has a great deal to say about that sub-human creature, mass man.

III

Of all the major anti-utopias of the first half of the twentieth century, in none does Wells appear to be more strikingly turned against himself than in Zamyatin's *We.* And this is something extremely important to understand, since the anti-utopian tradition after Wells pivots on *We.*

The setting for *We* is a Wellsian superstate of the twenty-sixth century, a giant city roofed with glass and cut off from the surrounding countryside by a great wall of glass:

This Green Wall is . . . the greatest invention ever conceived. Man ceased to be a wild animal the day he built the first wall; man ceased to be a wild man only on the day when the Green Wall was completed, when by this wall we isolated our machine-like, perfect world from the irrational, ugly world of trees, birds, and beasts. . . . (*We* 89)

In this city people live in great block apartments made of glass as strong as steel, a material used for everything from pavements to the *Integral,* the rocket ship being built to carry the perfection of the United State (or Single State, depending on the translation) to other worlds. Technology

99

has brought security of existence to the inhabitants of the glass city, who live on artificial food substances prepared from naphtha, and never have contact with nature outside the wall. The city, which is the United State, came into existence after the devastations of a Two Hundred Years' War.

Over this planned and controlled utopia rules the Well-Doer (also translated as Benefactor), a caricature of Lenin and a predecessor of Huxley's World Controller and Orwell's Big Brother, who makes every effort to take away troublesome human freedom and to reduce life to a perfect mathematical regularity. Citizens wear identical blue-gray uniforms, have numbers instead of names, march whenever possible in formations, and live as closely as they can by the Hour Tables, which regulate everything from the number of times a mouthful of food must be chewed to the hours of sleep required at night. The only opportunities for unregulated activity are the so-called Personal Hours, 1600-1700 and 2100-2300, when sexual intercourse, rationed by means of a state-issued checkbook of pink tickets, is permitted. Only at these times are people permitted to lower the curtains in their all-glass apartments: "Here and there in the huge mass of glass penetrated by sunshine there were grayish-blue squares, the opaque squares of lowered curtains, the squares of rhythmic, Taylorized happiness" (p. 41). Naturally in such a society art and literature are entirely instruments of the state, so that we learn of works like the immortal tragedy, "Those Who Come Late To Work," and the "Daily Odes to the Well-Doer."

But in spite of the Guardians, who watch constantly for any deviations, utilizing hovering aircraft and devices to overhear conversations, there is an attempt at revolt, and, as customary in anti-utopias, this involves love. The narrator, D-503, (the book is his diary) falls in love with I-330, the leader of an underground movement. The rebels are interested in winning D-503 to their cause since he is the builder of the *Integral*, which they hope to use to destroy the power of the state. Through love D-503 is transformed: he develops a soul and comes to understand—at least for a while—the rebels. When a riot takes place on the Day of Unanimity (when the Well-Doer is supposed to be unanimously "re-elected"), D-503 escapes with I-330 beyond the wall, where he encounters for the first time nature untouched by technology and civilization and meets primitive hairy men who have managed to survive since the great war. D-503 is overwhelmed by the contrast with the geometrical and antiseptic world within the Green Wall:

> The sun—it was no longer our light evenly diffused over the mirror surface of the pavements; it seemed an accumulation of living fragments, of incessantly oscillating, dizzy spots which blinded the eyes. And the trees! Like candles rising into the very sky, or like spiders that squatted upon the earth, supported by their clumsy paws, or like mute green fountains. And all this was moving, jumping, rustling. Under my feet some strange little ball was crawling. . . . I stood as though rooted to the ground. I was unable to take a step because under my foot there was not an even plane, but (imagine!) something disgustingly soft, yielding, living, springy, green! . . . (*We* 143–4)

But at the end of the novel, after the rebels fail to seize the *Integral*, D-503 undergoes an operation to remove the center of fancy, and he betrays I-330, then calmly sits by while she is tortured.

Ironically, Zamyatin, who spent eighteen months in England (1916–17), supervising the construction of Russian ice-breakers, and may have come to know Wells's work during that time, expressed great admiration for Wells in a slim book, *Herbert Wells*, published in 1922 and slightly revised in 1924.[21] The book provides the key to why *We* appears so anti-Wellsian.

What Zamyatin most admired about Wells was Wells's development of "social-scientific fantasy" (i.e. science fiction), which he considered to be Wells's great and original contribution, a contribution much more important than his realistic novels. For Zamyatin, Wells the realistic novelist was no more than a minor branch from the mighty trunk which was Dickens, but Wells the writer of social-scientific fantasy was one of the exceptionally talented few who have perfected or significantly changed literary form. In fact, Zamyatin felt that Wells in his social-scientific fantasy—his scientific romances—had almost alone created a new literary genre.

Zamyatin began his discussion of Wells's scientific romances by first pointing out that they are urban fairy tales. And just as the fairy tales of each and every country are drawn from the earth, the trees, the beasts of that land, so the scientific romances of Wells are drawn from the stony soil of the giant city of the twentieth century:

But imagine a country where the asphalt is the only fertile soil. On that soil, there is a dense jungle of only factory smokestacks; there are animals of only one breed—automobiles; and there is no spring fragrance except that of gasoline. This stony, asphalt, iron, gasoline, mechanical country is today's twentieth-century London, and, naturally, it should have grown its own iron and automobile goblins, produced its own mechanical and chemical fairy tales. Such tales exist: they have been told by Herbert Wells. They are his fantastic novels. (HW 105)

As urban fairy tales, the scientific romances of Wells are quite naturally based on the iron laws of science. Thus there is no magic in these fairy tales but only logic—of course, "logic more daring, more long-range than is normally found." And it is these iron laws of science which make Wells's fairy tales so plausible to the twentieth-century reader. At first, Zamyatin conceded, the combination of "an exact science and fairy tale, precision and fantasy," seems paradoxical. But on further investigation, it is not so at all. After all, myth—and Zamyatin considered these fairy tales myth—"is always, visibly or invisibly, bound with religion." And "the religion of today's city," Zamyatin pointed out, "is exact science" (p. 107).

But Wells's scientific romances are much more than the fairy tales of a mechanical and scientific age. An element of social criticism, Zamyatin insisted, is also woven into each of them: "No matter what fairy tale Wells may be telling, no matter how far, at first glance, the tale may seem removed from social problems, the reader will be inevitably brought to these problems" (p. 114). In the "cruel mirror of Wellsian fantasy," we see the monstrous, ironical reflection of our own social maladies: Wells has unfailingly alloyed social satire to his scientific fantasy (p. 142).

Finally, Zamyatin refined his definition of the Wellsian social-scientific fantasy by contrasting it with utopian fiction. There are, he said, "two generic and unchanging characteristics of utopia":

One of them lies in the content. The authors of utopias present what to them appear to be ideal social structures. Or, if we translate into the language of mathematics, utopias have a plus sign. The other characteristic, emerging organically from the content, is in the form: a utopia is always static, a utopia is always a description and does not contain—or almost does not contain—the dynamics of a plot. (HW 141)

Almost nowhere in Wells's social-scientific fantasy, Zamyatin believed, can one find these characteristics:

He uses his social fantasy novels almost exclusively to uncover the defects of the existing social order, not to create a picture of some paradise to come. In his predictions, there is not a single rosy or golden glimmer of paradise, but, rather, the somber colors of Goya. And the very same Goya is in *The Time Machine, The First Men in the Moon, The War in the Air,* and *The World Set Free.* Only in one of the weakest social fantasy novels of Wells, *Men Like Gods*, will we see the sweet, pink colors of utopia. (*HW* 141) [22]

Herbert Wells also proves then that, however others may have regarded him, Zamyatin did not think of Wells as the advocate of a regimented utopian perfection which would tyrannize over the soul of man. On the contrary, we see in *Herbert Wells* that Zamyatin honored Wells for belonging to the tiny elite of heretics whose function is to lead mankind into the future. Who these most valuable of men are is best understood in terms of Zamyatin's concepts of entropy and energy, concepts stated in *We* and in two articles, "Tomorrow" and "On Literature, Revolution, and Entropy."

"There are two forces in the world," says I-330 in *We*, "entropy and energy. One leads into blessed quietude, to happy equilibrium, the other to the destruction of equilibrium, to torturingly perpetual motion" (p. 153). Energy manifests itself in human affairs in the form of revolution; revolution, in its turn, can never be final, for it is only one stage in a constant dialectical process. Most men (the great majority, whom Zamyatin called the "live-dead") accept as "absolute truth and as living principles the conventions and dogmas" of the last stage in the dialectical process. Opposed to them are a tiny group of heretics (the "live-live"), men like Wells who leap into today from tomorrow and lead the world to the next stage in the dialectical process. Indeed, all great artists are heretics, and to combat man's chronic disease of entropy is the chief function of literature.

It is not hard, then, to explain what has happened in *We*. Zamyatin, himself an artist-heretic, took the Wellsian social-scientific fantasy and used it as a vehicle for his attack on the way in which the Soviet Union was betraying the principles of the Revolution. Rigidly righteous in following dogma, the Soviets were killing men in order to save mankind. As Marc

Slonim remarked, "Zamyatin simply could not call what he saw around him a revolution: doctrine encrusting the lava of rebellion, the bloodthirsty executions, the stupid regimentation, the creation of ideocracy in lieu of autocracy." [23] And because he took so much from Wells—not only the form but details—and because the State he pictured is intended by its Well-Doer to be a utopia, *We* comes out seemingly anti-Wellsian in its anti-utopianism. In fact *We* appears so anti-Wellsian that one could easily classify it with works like *"The Machine Stops"* and *Brave New World*, whose authors admitted to having started out to attack the Wellsian vision of utopia.[24]

Actually, Zamyatin probably did not understand the drift of Wells's work well enough to see that the rationalism and regimentation he opposed in *We* was at least a strong element in Wells's thought. In *We* Zamyatin wrote more of a critique of Wells than he probably ever realized, a critique which has been very strongly influenced by Dostoevsky's fulmination against reason and the idea of the perfectibility of man in *Notes From Underground*. D-503's discovery that the irrational, symbolized by $\sqrt{-1}$, exists is much the same as the underground man's belief that "two times two makes four is no longer life, gentlemen, but is the beginning of death." Even the possibility of reducing life to mathematical entries in the Hour Tables can be found foreshadowed in *Notes From Underground*, particularly in this passage:

All human actions will then, of course, be tabulated according to these laws, mathematically, like tables of logarithms up to 108,000, and entered in a table; or, better still, there would be published certain edifying works like the present encyclopedic lexicons, in which everything will be so clearly calculated and designated that there will be no more incidents or adventures in the world.[25]

Finally, the underground man's crystal palace looks forward to the glass city of the United State.

But for our purposes the most striking aspect of *We* is the great extent to which Zamyatin borrowed many important details and images from Wells's scientific romances—details and images which in their turn were taken from Zamyatin by anti-utopian writers like Orwell. Zamyatin was particularly indebted to Wells's picture of the world in 2100 as portrayed in *When the Sleeper Wakes* and "A Story of the Days To Come," works which he praised as the most magnificent, the most ironic of "Wellsian grotesques." There are, of course, significant differences between Wells's world of 2100 and Zamyatin's world of 2500—for example, Zamyatin's is much more of a classless world than is Wells's, and there are no traces of capitalism in it, though one can easily imagine *We* as an evolution from *When the Sleeper Wakes* and "A Story of the Days To Come."

Zamyatin's most obvious—and most important—indebtedness to Wells was for the image of the supercity, what Wells described in *When the Sleeper Wakes* and "A Story of the Days To Come" as the "complex mechanical city" that "had swallowed up mankind." And to illustrate the features of the Wellsian supercity—"a preternaturally enlarged mechanical beehive"—we need to quote again the passage from *When the Sleeper Wakes*:

His first impression was of overwhelming architecture. The place into which he looked was an aisle of Titanic buildings, curving spaciously in either direction. Overhead mighty cantilevers sprang together across the huge width of the place, and a tracery of translucent material shut out the sky. Gigantic globes of cold white shamed the pale sunbeams that filtered down through the girders and wires. Here and there a gossamer suspension bridge dotted with foot passengers flung across the chasm and the air was webbed with slender cables. A cliff of edifice hung above him, he perceived, as he glanced upward, and the opposite façade was grey and dim and broken by great archings, circular perforations, balconies, buttresses, turret projections, myriads of vast windows, and an intricate scheme of architectural relief. (WSW 28)

One needs only add to this description that this great glass-roofed mechanical city ends abruptly in a great wall, outside of which lies the now uninhabited countryside. In essential features this is also the city in *We*: glass-covered, mechanically complex, sealed off from nature by the Green Wall.

The giant mechanical city represents for both Wells and Zamyatin the victory of the city over the land. Where Wells had the giant city come into existence as the consequence of a peaceful evolution, Zamyatin made it a literal victory of the city over the land in a Two Hundred Years' War. Zamyatin was here clearly indebted to another cluster of Wellsian ideas about the future which, as we have seen before, are set forth in other of Wells's scientific romances, particularly in *The War in the Air* and *The World Set Free*. Zamyatin discussed these ideas at some length in *Herbert Wells*: the prediction of world destruction by war, resulting in the collapse of civilization and a return to barbarism, followed in its turn by the building of the World State out of the ruins of the old order by an elite of functional men.

We seems to show further indebtedness to Wells in the rebellion led by I-330 and her friends against the regimentation of the great mechanical city of the United State. For this rebellion there is a prototype in *When the Sleeper Wakes*. Wells's story similarly comes to a climax with a rebellion, in this case when the blue-clad workers rise, under the direction of Graham the sleeper, against their leaders. At the end of both *When the Sleeper Wakes* and *We* the outcome of the rebellion is in doubt—another detail for which Zamyatin could well have been indebted to Wells. The attempt of the rebels to seize the rocket ship *Integral* is surely suggested by the attempt of the revolutionaries in Wells's novel to capture the stages from which airplanes come and go.

Two of the most important acts of defiance by Zamyatin's rebels against the regimentation of the mechanical city have their originals in another Wellsian story, "A Story of the Days To Come." D-503's love for I-330, which is in last analysis a "political act," may have been suggested by the love of Elizabeth and Denton in "A Story of the Days To Come," a love which is in essence also an act of defiance against the state and the system. And to escape the system and live free, Elizabeth and Denton try for a time to survive outside the city in the uninhabited country—clearly the model for the rebels' going outside the Green Wall to nature. Unfamiliar as they are with anything beyond the high walls of the giant city, their first reactions to nature are like those of D-503 in his first visit outside the Green Wall. "Come out and see the clouds," Elizabeth cries.

Besides these major similarities, there are many other minor echoes in *We* of *When the Sleeper Wakes* and "A Story of the Days To Come." Thus, the Guardians are descended from Wells's Labour Police; the operation on D-503's brain to remove fancy from Wells's "psychic surgery"; the phono-lecturers from the Babble Machines; the Child Educational Refinery from the mechanical crèches; the numbered uniforms of the citizens of the United State from the numbered blue canvas suits of the Labour Company slaves; the structural glass, out of which so many things are made, from the *Integral* to apartment houses, from "the recently invented glass-like substance" used to roof over London. Even the Ancient House has its prototype in the survival of St. Paul's and other old buildings—"embedded out of sight, arched over and covered in among the giant growths of this great age."

In addition to all these and doubtless many other indebtednesses to *When the Sleeper Wakes* and "A Story of the Days To Come," one could find in *We*, I think, echoes of other of Wells's science fiction besides the indebtednesses to *The War in the Air* and *The World Set Free,* which we have already noted. For example, Zamyatin's fear that communism would degenerate into "a new State slavery, well-planned and inescapable," could have found an effective symbol in the lunar ant heap of *The First Men in the Moon,* where the Selenite is conditioned and adapted to his function in society. *We* is overwhelmingly a Wellsian social-scientific fantasy.

I should add as an epilogue to this discussion that there is a very slight possibility that "The Machine Stops" could have influenced *We,* since Forster's story was first published in 1909 and Zamyatin might have read it when he was in England in 1916–17. After all, both *We* and "The Machine Stops" are remarkably similar as to the mechanical quality of the life they predict. But there is no evidence from *Herbert Wells,* where Zamyatin mentioned others who followed Wells in writing social-scientific fantasy, that he had even heard of "The Machine Stops," so that the similarities between the two works should probably be explained by the common influence of Wells.

In this connection it is interesting to note that in *Herbert Wells* Zamyatin identified his own *We* with the kind of social-scientific fantasy he saw Wells as having invented. After pointing out that the petrified life of the old, pre-revolutionary Russia could hardly have produced this kind of fantasy, he goes on to say that new conditions have begun to make such fantasy possible:

But post-revolutionary Russia, having become the most fantastic of modern European countries, will doubtless mirror this period of her history in literary fantasy. And there is already a beginning of this: *Aelita* and *Hyperboloid* by A. N. Tolstoy; *We,* a novel by the author of this article. . . . (*HW* 146)

CHAPTER VI

T HE TWO MOST famous anti-utopias, at least in the
English-speaking world, are *Brave New World* (1932)
and *Nineteen Eighty-four* (1949), works which, though they
are each unique, are also strangely similar. Both seem to
represent a development, not only from *We* but also from
"The Machine Stops," and in this respect they seem to
define in a rough way, one early and the other late, a second
wave in the anti-utopian reaction. Perhaps the best way to
describe the difference between the first and second wave—
an admittedly subtle and elusive difference—is to say that
with the second wave the anti-utopia moves another step
away from the mythic toward the satiric, a movement
roughly parallel to the shift in Wells's writings from, say,

The Time Machine to *When the Sleeper Wakes*. At the same time these anti-utopias are still Wellsian science fiction, and essentially hostile to the Wellsian vision of utopia, though in the case of *Nineteen Eighty-four* the explanation of this opposition is not simple and straightforward.

Many years after writing *Brave New World,* Huxley told an interviewer for the *Paris Review* that his famous book had "started out as a parody of H. G. Wells's *Men Like Gods,* but gradually it got out of hand and turned into something quite different from what I'd originally intended." [1] Though it became a "Pyrhonnic esthete's" nauseated rejection of the modern world, it remained—sometimes consciously, at other times unconsciously—a parody of the Wellsian vision. As such, not only was it a manifestation of the reaction against "progress" which set in among intellectuals after World War I, but it was also closely akin in its anti-machine bias to Forster's "The Machine Stops." And it became such a twentieth-century classic that few educated people would need to be reminded of the features of its mechanical paradise of sex and soma, decanted embryos and conditioned adults, where social stability is achieved by taking away troublesome human freedom and stifling all strong emotions:

. . . no leisure from pleasure, not a moment to sit down and think—or if ever by some unlucky chance such a crevice of time should yawn in the solid substance of their distractions, there is always *soma,* delicious *soma,* half a gramme for a half-holiday, a gramme for a week-end, two grammes for a trip to the gorgeous East, three for a dark eternity on the moon; returning whence they find themselves on the other side of the crevice, safe on the solid ground of daily labour and distraction, scampering from feely to feely, from girl to pneumatic girl, from Electromagnetic Golf course to. . . . (*BNW* 67)

As a parody of the Wellsian vision, *Brave New World* is throughout quite heavily indebted to Wells and not solely to

Men Like Gods. Most obviously the world of A.F. 600 is Wells's World State (Huxley even borrowed the phrase), what Wells described in *The Open Conspiracy* as "a single world commonweal, preventing war and controlling those moral, biological and economic forces that would otherwise lead to wars." And this World State comes into existence after a series of events familiar to us from Wells's future histories, *The War in the Air, The World Set Free,* and *The Shape of Things To Come:* the Nine Years' War begun in A.F. 141 is followed by the great Economic Collapse, when mankind is left with a choice between World Control or total destruction. And the conditioning and genetic determination, so essential to the stability of Huxley's World State, are themes in Wells's utopias and romances, going back at least as far as *The First Men in the Moon,* a work Huxley confessed to admiring and one which is very clearly a prototype of *Brave New World.* Huxley's State Conditioning Centres are the crèches in *When the Sleeper Wakes* and "A Story of the Days To Come."

Other indebtednesses are also very evident. The islands for nonconformists, to which Bernard Marx and Helmholtz Watson are finally sent, are the islands for criminals and social misfits in *A Modern Utopia.* The colored class-marking uniforms of the Gammas, Deltas, and Epsilons derive from the blue canvas of the Labour Company in *When the Sleeper Wakes* and "A Story of the Days To Come." Furthermore, a list of details, not necessarily Wellsian in origin but Wellsian in spirit, would be very long indeed: including synthetic music machines, reading machines, and scent organs; steel and rubber benches in the parks; rocket planes, helicopters, and monorail trains; the pink glass tower of the Abortion Centre; phosphorus recovery at the Slough Crematorium, and the aluminum hat in which a reporter carries his wireless receiver and transmitter. And surely something of the feel of the Wellsian scientific romance can be detected in the famous description of the Fertilizing Room which appears at the beginning of the novel:

The enormous room on the ground floor faced towards the north. Cold for all the summer beyond the panes, for all the tropical heat of the room itself, a harsh thin light glared through the windows, hungrily seeking some draped lay figure, some pallid shape of academic goose-flesh, but finding only the glass and nickel and bleakly shining porcelain of a laboratory. Wintriness responded to wintriness. The over-alls of the workers were white, their hands gloved with a pale corpse-coloured rubber. The light was frozen, dead, a ghost. Only from the yellow barrels of the microscopes did it borrow a certain rich and living substance, lying along the polished tubes like butter, streak after luscious streak in long recession down the work tables. (*BNW* 1–2)

And certainly *Brave New World* is anti-Wellsian,[2] and very naturally so. In the years previous to writing *Brave New World*, Huxley often demonstrated his distaste for the Wellsian vision: thus, for example, the brilliant caricature, quoted above from *Point Counter Point*, of the Wellsian utopia spiraling off to infinity. And as John Atkins has pointed out, Huxley often speculated about the future in many of his novels, foreshadowing aspects of *Brave New World* at least as far back as *Crome Yellow* and Scogan's Rational State with its vast state nurseries, and Francis Chelifer's millennium when slavery would be really scientific and efficient.[3] But even more important than the novels in anticipating his great anti-utopia are Huxley's essays. Particularly in certain essays written during the decade before *Brave New World* we can see the maturing of the anti-Wellsian distrust of machines and material progress which so much animates *Brave New World*.

First, there is Huxley's disbelief in the possibility of

progress. In "Progress: How the Achievements of Civilization Will Eventually Bankrupt the Entire World" (1928), he wrote:

Uninheritable progress, due to tradition, has genuinely taken place in the realm of science and technology, where each worker stands on the shoulders of his predecessors. In the realm of morals, the refinement of traditional codes may lead to a certain ethical progress throughout a whole society. But the greater part of what is called moral progress consists merely in changes that are entirely without ameliorative direction. Progress in the arts is very limited and, as soon as the technique of artistic expression is perfected, ceases altogether to exist.[4]

This, of course, was Huxley in his dilettante phase, still debunking everyone and everything. He naturally saw the development of the doctrine of progress as having been made inevitable by the "enormous expansion of man's material resources during the age of industrialism," and, quoting Ben Jonson, he cautioned against the pernicious doctrine:

> It is not growing like a tree
> In bulk doth make men better be.

But in spite of Ben Jonson's warning, this is precisely what we have fondly imagined. Because we use a hundred and ten times as much coal as our ancestors, we believe ourselves a hundred and ten times better, intellectually, morally and spiritually.[5]

Then there is Huxley's distrust of the machine. For example, in "On Making Things Too Easy: How Modern Inventions and Distractions May Assist in Inducing Mental Decay" (1926), "Machinery, Psychology, and Politics" (1929), and "Spinoza's Worm" (1929), he rehearsed some of the classic anti-machine arguments we have seen in "The Machine Stops." Huxley argued that the machine dehumanizes men by demanding mechanical efficiency of them and that it limits aesthetic choice by providing only standardized articles, but most important, that the machine is one of the great menaces to modern life because it makes creativity unnecessary and robs the majority of human beings of the very possibility of happiness. Even leisure has been mechanized:

Men no longer amuse themselves, creatively, but sit and are passively amused by mechanical devices. Machinery condemns one of the most vital needs of humanity to a frustration which the progress of invention can only render more and more complete.[6]

And so men come to seek the lowest, which is "copiously provided by the film-makers, the newspaper proprietors, the broadcasters, and all the rest." [7]

It is interesting to note here that Orwell recognized—and applauded—*Brave New World* as an anti-machine answer to Wells:

And in any book by anyone who feels at home in the machine-world—in any book by H. G. Wells, for instance—you will find passages of the same kind. How often have we not heard it, that glutinously uplifting stuff about "the machines, our new race of slaves, which will set humanity free," etc., etc., etc. To these people, apparently, the only danger of the machine is its possible use for destructive purposes; as, for instance, aeroplanes are used in war. Barring wars and unforeseen disaster, the future is envisaged as an ever more rapid march of mechanical progress; machines to save work, machines to save thought, machines to save pain, hygiene, efficiency, organization, more hygiene, more efficiency, more organisation, more machines—until finally you land up in the by now familiar Wellsian Utopia, aptly caricatured by Huxley in *Brave New World*, the paradise of little fat men. Of course in their daydreams of the future the little fat men are neither fat nor little; they are Men Like Gods.[8]

But the essay that is most important in revealing the anti-Wellsian beliefs on which *Brave New World* is written is "Boundaries of Utopia" (1932), a vigorous attack on the machine-produced utopia. Huxley led into his attack by arguing that Lord Acton was wrong when he said that modern liberty differs from medieval in not being dependent on property. On the contrary, wrote Huxley, legal liberties are, in practice, just as dependent on property as ever: "The rich can buy large quantities of freedom; the poor must do without it." But in the future, say the prophets of utopia,

"three hundred a year will buy five thousand pounds' worth of liberty." And when we ask how, by what miracle? they invoke, not the god from the machine, but the machine itself.[9]

For the machine, wrote Huxley, is the "only 'other person' at whose expense we can have things with a good conscience and also the only 'other person' who becomes steadily more and more efficient."

And then Huxley described the mechanical utopia to come, in a paragraph which obviously echoes the Wellsian vision:

Served by mechanical domestics, exploiting the incessant labour of metallic slaves, the three-hundred-a-year man of the future state will enjoy an almost indefinite leisure. A system of transport, rapid, frequent, and cheap, will enable him to move about the globe more freely than the migrant *rentier* of the present age. Nor need he forgo (except in private) the rich man's privilege of living luxuriously. Already mass production has made it possible for the relatively poor to enjoy elaborate entertainments in surroundings of more than regal splendour. The theatres in which the egalitarians will enjoy the talkies, tasties, smellies, and feelies, the Corner Houses where they will eat their synthetic poached eggs on toast-substitute and drink their surrogates of coffee, will be prodigiously much vaster and more splendid than anything we know today. Compared with them, the hall of Belshazzar in Martin's celebrated picture will seem the squalidest of little chop houses and Bibbiena's palaces, Piranesi's imaginary Roman temples, mere dogholes, hutches and sties.[10]

With its talk of the rapid, globe-encircling system of transport and the titanic utopian architecture, this passage obviously derives from Wells, particularly from A *Modern Utopia*, where travel becomes the common texture of life. It also echoes the giant city of *When the Sleeper Wakes* and

"A Story of the Days To Come." At the same time, with its mention of talkies, tasties, smellies, and feelies and its synthetic poached eggs and surrogates of coffee, it directly foreshadows *Brave New World*. It is as though one were looking into the alembic while Huxley was distilling *Brave New World*.

Huxley made it plain that he did not like this egalitarian state. His chief worry was that when everybody in the future enjoys abundance and leisure, life won't be worth living for anybody. To establish his point, he invoked "The Law of Diminishing Returns" to prove that the "prophets" (e.g. H. G. Wells) were absolutely wrong when they said that "Perfected machinery will give us increasing freedom from work, and increasing freedom from work will give increasing happiness." On the contrary, Huxley believed that leisure will become misery, and even travel will no longer be educative:

But the more traveling there is, the more will culture and way of life tend everywhere to be standardized and therefore the less educative will travel become. There is still some point in going from Burslem to Udaipur. But when all the inhabitants of Burslem have been sufficiently often to Udaipur and all the inhabitants of Udaipur have been sufficiently often to Burslem, there will be no point whatever in making the journey. Leaving out of account a few trifling geological and climatic idiosyncrasies the two towns will have become essentially indistinguishable.[11]

Nature, of course, will be ruined when everyone can go to the country. So, as usual at this time, Huxley ended up attacking the idea of increasing the happiness of the people.

It is not surprising that Huxley started *Brave New World* as a parody of *Men Like Gods*, and, although Huxley spoke of the work growing under his pen and becoming something else, he in fact stuck very much with his original intention —perhaps more unconsciously than consciously—and the work was to a great extent devoted to showing, by exaggeration and caricature, what Huxley thought the Wellsian utopia would really be like. It is Wellsian in form, too, as at least one contemporary, Alan Reynolds Thompson, realized in his review in the *Bookman*, March, 1932: ". . . it has a general scheme like that of an H. G. Wells romance." [12] Again we are in the presence of Wellsian science fiction used to attack the Wellsian vision.

Brave New World truly catches the distinctive character of the Wellsian vision presented in *Men Like Gods*. But *Men Like Gods* is closer to Skinner's *Walden Two* than to *A Modern Utopia*. In *Men Like Gods* the psychologist has taken the place of the policeman and men are taught—Wells does not use the word "conditioned," because the word did not enter the popular vocabulary until after Pavlov's book in 1928—to be good. In fact, government has withered away and there are only experts and citizens who have been successfully educated: "Utopia has no parliament, no politics, no private wealth, no business competition, no police nor prisons, no lunatics, no defectives nor cripples." The slogan of the men like gods—"Education is our government"—is obviously being parodied in the education by conditioning of the citizens of *Brave New World*. Because of Wells's enthusiastic praise for Pavlov's *Conditioned Reflexes* and because of his defense of the book against the attacks of Shaw, it must have been easy for Huxley to associate conditioning with Wells.[13]

Huxley's chief strategy was to show that the conditioned happiness of *Brave New World* cuts men off from deep experience, keeps them from being fully human. This is a familiar twentieth-century objection to utopia, and its most important flaw is that it sees no middle ground between misery and total control and planning. The black-white nature of this antithesis is brilliantly caught in the famous concluding remarks of the interview between John the Savage and the World Controller, Mustapha Mond. John is talking:

"But I don't want comfort. I want God, I want poetry, I want real danger, I want freedom, I want goodness. I want sin."

"In fact," said Mustapha Mond, "You're claiming the right to be unhappy."

"Not to mention the right to grow old and ugly and impotent; the right to have syphilis and cancer; the right to have too little to eat; the right to be lousy; the right to live in constant apprehension of what may happen tomorrow; the right to catch typhoid; the right to be tortured by unspeakable pains of every kind."

There was a long silence.

"I claim them all," said the Savage at last.

Mustapha Mond shrugged his shoulders. "You're welcome," he said. (*BNW* 288)

But in spite of the fact that Huxley could obviously see the other side,[14] he offered John the Savage no reasonable alternative from which to choose: only the insanity of utopia and the lunacy of the reservation. In *Island* we are finally given a third possibility.

It is interesting to note that, in the debate between Rupert Catskill and Urthred in *Men Like Gods*, Wells anticipated Huxley's very objections in *Brave New World*. "Because our life is dreadfuller," says Catskill, "it has, and it must have, moments that are infinitely brighter than yours. It is titanic, Sir, where this is merely tidy" (p. 82). Huxley might substitute "trivial" for "tidy," but essentially this is his position. And as we have seen earlier, Wells adequately met the Huxleyan objections by showing that a way of human living is possible which can be "steadfast and disciplined and at the same time vigorous and happy." Utopia need hardly be, he showed, a passive and static thing—its seeming calm is deceptive:

He had always thought of Utopia as a tranquility with everything settled for good. Even to-day it seemed tranquil under that level haze, but he knew that this quiet was the steadiness of a mill race, which seems almost motionless in its quiet onrush until a bubble or fleck of foam or some stick or leaf shoots along it and reveals its velocity. (*MLG* 140)

But, of course, *Brave New World* is by no means fully explained when we have shown the astonishing extent to which it is a counterthrust to Wells. Indeed, many critics have seen it exclusively as a brilliant satire of tendencies Huxley saw in the world around him. As such it is the work of the Huxley who was still nauseated by most human beings, the same Huxley who wrote these words in *Antic Hay*: "The way they breed. Like maggots, Sir, like maggots. Millions of them creeping about the face of the country, spreading blight and dirt wherever they go, ruining every-thing. It's the people I object to. . . ." [15] And it is the same Huxley who lets the cat out of the bag when he speaks of the "infinitely precious experience of being in a superior minority" in the last sentence of "Boundaries of Utopia."

Indeed, the distinctive flavor of *Brave New World* results from the fact that it was written by a cynical, bored young man who felt the contempt of his class for the machine. He was against utopia not only because it would mechanize human life but because it would give abundance and leisure to everyone, making these no longer the special privilege of people like himself. Needless to say, this aspect of *Brave New World* produced angry responses from leftist critics of the 1930's, such as the following from Granville Hicks in a review in *The New Republic*:

With war in Asia, bankruptcy in Europe and starvation everywhere, what do you suppose Aldous Huxley is now worrying about? If you happen to have read an article he published about a year ago in *The Virginia Quarterly Review* ["Boundaries of Utopia"], you will be able to guess. He is worrying about the unpleasantness of life in the utopia that, as he sees it, is just a century or two ahead.[16]

Wells in *The Shape of Things To Come* called Huxley "a brilliant reactionary."

But before leaving Huxley we should briefly look at two works which also show Wellsian influence and which relate to *Brave New World*—*Ape and Essence* (1946) and *Island* (1962). Sixteen years after *Brave New World*, Huxley still found Wellsian science fiction viable as a vehicle for social criticism in *Ape and Essence*, a work which, though far more sincere in its criticisms and far more bitter in its denunciations, is far less successful as a work of art. But it is every bit as much a Wellsian romance, and, as such, it provides major confirmation of Wells's impact on Huxley.

Ape and Essence is a post-catastrophe novel in the classic manner. In the year 2108, the New Zealand Rediscovery Expedition to North America lands at El Segundo, where its chief Botanist is captured by the backward people who live in the ruins of Los Angeles. They are the familiar descendants of the survivors of the great disaster, affected by radioactivity and the diseases released by bacteriological warfare. Most of the population has become animal-like, mating only during a short rutting season of a few weeks. Children are usually born deformed, and those who exceed a certain limit of deformity (more than seven fingers, for example) are sacrificed in a bloody ritual dedicated to Belial, who is now worshipped instead of God. The people barely wrest a living from the depleted soil, digging up corpses to find clothes and burning books to bake their bread. At the end the New Zealand botanist escapes with a native girl to a colony of "Hots" who live to the north near Fresno. The Hots are people who still mate in the normal human fashion, and, as a result, apparently maintain some of the old dignity of human life.

But although it is Wellsian science fiction, *Ape and Essence* is hardly an attack on the Wellsian vision in the manner of *Brave New World*. Indeed, it could hardly be so in view of how Huxley had matured to a more fully human sympathy in the sixteen years since *Brave New World*. *Ape and Essence* is primarily a warning of how men, disregarding even their own self-interest, have set themselves in a direction which will lead ultimately to their own destruction. Either men, reproducing without limit and plundering their own planet, will eventually starve to death, or, more likely, they will turn their own technology loose and ravage the world in a great holocaust. Behind it all—and in this respect *Ape and Essence* could be considered anti-Wellsian—lies man's pride in setting himself against the Order of Things: "From the very beginning of the industrial revolution [Belial] foresaw that men would be made so overweeningly bumptious by the miracles of their own technology that they would soon lose all sense of reality." [17]

In *Island* Huxley offered the alternative to the insanity of the World State and the lunacy of the reservation, the alternative which, as a "Pyrhonnic aesthete," he had excluded from *Brave New World*. Although *Island* is dull and lifeless as fiction, it is a serious, carefully conceived projection of an ideal society. Significantly, the twentieth century's most brilliant anti-utopian turned to the utopia, the favorite Wellsian form he once ridiculed, for his final vision of a good human life. And as Geoffrey Gorer has pointed out, Huxley was like Wells in being a utopia builder who had read widely in biology, physiology, and psychology.[18]

The Huxleyan utopia, naturally enough, is quite different from the Wellsian. Technology is viewed with suspicion, and great effort is made to control its development on Pala, the island home of utopia. Then Huxley, unlike Wells, makes psychological, spiritual, and physical health, rather than human achievement and mastery of the universe, the supreme value of his utopia. In presenting different utopian ends, *Island* in a way is more subtly anti-Wellsian than *Brave New World*.

But most important, *Island* is the mature and responsible Huxley's answer to *Brave New World*. Where there was once *soma* to prevent men and women from feeling deeply, there is now *moksha*, the hallucinogen, which brings mystical vision; where there was once promiscuous sex to provide escape, there is now the yoga of sex, a road to enlightenment; where there was once Bokanovskification, there is now voluntary artificial insemination to raise the quality of the population. Now, instead of destroying the family, there are Mutual Adoption Clubs of many adults and children—a kind of extended family—wherein each child can grow to maturity without developing neuroses and distortions of personality. Instead of the ever-increasing consumption of material goods, there is now electricity, light industry, and agriculture to provide security of means; instead of Alphas, Betas, Gammas, Deltas, and Epsilons, there is now somatyping to nip in the bud potential Hitlers and Stalins. In *Island*, everything is done to provide what Huxley called for in 1946 in the Introduction to *Brave New World:*

In this community economics would be decentralist and Henry-Georgian, politics Kropotkinesque and co-operative. Science and technology would be used as though, like the Sabbath, they had been made for man, not (as at present and still more so in the Brave New World) as though man were to be adapted and enslaved to them. Religion would be the conscious and intelligent pursuit of man's Final End, the unitive knowledge of the immanent Tao or Logos, the transcendent Godhead or Brahman.[19]

II

By 1947, when Orwell was writing *Nineteen Eighty-four* against a background of totalitarianism, dreams of reason— no matter how Wellsian—were no longer reasonable or appropriate subjects for ridicule. So instead of a caricature like that in Huxley's work, anti-Wellsianism in *Nineteen Eighty-four* takes the form of an expansion of Orwell's criticism in "Wells, Hitler and the World State." In that essay Orwell noted that Wells was too sane and rational to understand Hitler, nationalism, and militarism. Similarly, the Wellsian vision of a great World State where men have joined together to apply reason and the scientific method to human problems, where men no longer derive pleasure from violence and power, is unrealistic. Given human nature and the managerial revolution, we should rather look forward to something like *Nineteen Eighty-four*, where an elite of talent pursues power for its own sake and the image of the future is "a boot stamping on a human face forever." In its denial of reason and empiricism, in its collective solipsism that can assert that $2 + 2 = 5$, and in its refined sadism and cruelty, the world of *Nineteen Eighty-four* is the complete antithesis of the Wellsian vision. O'Brien torturing Winston Smith in the cellars of the Ministry of Love, said Orwell, is what we shall have, not a utopia of reason where men are like Gods.

But while *Nineteen Eighty-four* shifts the emphasis in its attack against Wells from what we find in other anti-utopias, it is every bit as much Wellsian science fiction. "*Nineteen Eighty-four*," as Wyndham Lewis has written, "is Wellsian in form, Wellsian in the style of its writing, Wellsian in the colourlessness and anonymity of its personae." In other words, it is "a prophetic Wellsian nightmare of events in the future." [20] I would dispute the estimate of Wells's and Orwell's powers of characterization, but essentially Lewis is right. In fact, *Nineteen Eighty-four* is, as we will see later, a lineal descendant of two particular Wellsian romances, *When the Sleeper Wakes* and "A Story of the Days To Come."

None of this is surprising, since Orwell knew Wells's writings very well and, in his youth and early maturity, would have agreed with his hero George Bowling in *Coming*

Up For Air, for whom Wells was the author who had made the greatest impression. Elsewhere Orwell spoke of reading and re-reading the entire published work of Wells, while his testimonial to the impact of Wells on people born about the turn of the century is further evidence of Wells's importance.[21] Orwell several times analyzed Wells, most extensively in "Wells, Hitler and the World State," Chapter XII of *The Road to Wigan Pier*, and "The True Pattern of H. G. Wells."

Orwell not only recognized Wells's enormous influence up to 1914, but he also admired the fiction of Wells's most creative period, 1895 to 1910. For everything from scientific romances to comedies of lower-middle-class life, the adjective Orwell most used was "brilliant." But after World War I, Orwell detected a decline in Wells's power as artist as well as a loss in the significance of his message to his contemporaries. It was the familiar story: like other intellectuals after World War I, Orwell suffered a revulsion against "progress," which he identified with Wells. And, although it is not revealed in *Nineteen Eighty-four*, Orwell, like the others, came to dislike the Wellsian vision, though his dislike was much more temperate and sane. For Orwell progress meant chiefly mechanical progress; and accordingly his attitude toward Wells was intimately connected with his bias against the machine, a bias he did his very best to exorcise but could never completely be rid of. The fullest statement of this distrust of the machine and the Wellsian utopia is in Chapter XII of *The Road to Wigan Pier* and reveals that if Orwell had written *Nineteen Eighty-four* in the 1930's instead of in 1949, it would have been another *Brave New World*.

Orwell came to the discussion of the machine in an effort to win support for socialism. Many sensitive people, he had discovered, recoil from socialism because the "idea of Socialism is bound up, more or less inextricably, with the idea of machine-production." So he attempted to show that one doesn't need to be a machine-lover to be a socialist. Certainly he himself was not.

Of course, only a fool, he admitted, would talk about scrapping the machine since "the machine has come to stay." And one must understand that as long as there are people starving in the world, as long as there are men breaking their backs digging ditches, it would be inhuman even to think of Erewhonian machine-breaking. Still, hostility is a healthy attitude, and, although the machine had to be accepted, "it is probably better to accept it rather as one accepts a drug—that is, grudgingly and suspiciously."

In describing the "glittering Wells-world" so often identified with the future to be brought by Socialism, Orwell revealed the hostilities to machinery we have seen to be characteristic of Forster and Huxley:

> Where there is one aeroplane now, in those days there will be fifty! All the work that is now done by hand will then be done by machinery; everything that is now made of leather, wood or stone will be made of rubber, glass or steel; there will be no loose ends, no wildernesses, no wild animals, no weeds, no disease, no poverty, no pain—and so on and so forth. The Socialist world is to be above all things an *ordered* world, an *efficient* world. But it is precisely from that vision of the future as a sort of glittering Wells-world that sensitive minds recoil.[22]

Later these hostilities became more explicit.

At heart, though he believed the machine must be accepted, Orwell felt convinced of "the tendency of the machine to make a fully human life impossible." The machine is the enemy of life, and progress is a swindle because it will create a "paradise of little fat men." And Wells's Men Like Gods theory is no answer:

> All mechanical progress is towards greater and greater efficiency; ultimately, therefore, towards a world in which *nothing goes wrong.*

But in a world in which nothing went wrong, many of the qualities which Mr. Wells regards as "godlike" would be no more valuable than the animal faculty of moving the ears. The beings in *Men Like Gods* and *The Dream* are represented, for example, as brave, generous and physically strong. But in a world from which physical danger has been banished—and obviously mechanical progress tends to eliminate danger—would physical courage be likely to survive? *Could* it survive? And why should physical strength survive in a world where there was never the need for physical labour? As for such qualities as loyalty, generosity, etc., in a world where nothing went wrong, they would be not only irrelevant but probably unimaginable. The truth is that many of the qualities we admire in human beings can only function in opposition to some kind of disaster, pain or difficulty; but the tendency of mechanical progress is to eliminate disaster, pain and difficulty.[23]

Thus Orwell feared all mechanical progress as "a frantic struggle towards an objective which you hope and pray will never be reached," a struggle to achieve a world in which all need for human effort and creation will be ended. "The logical end of mechanical progress," he wrote, "is to reduce the human brain to something resembling a brain in a bottle." [24]

But, much as he distrusts the machine and the Wellsian utopia, it is not these which Orwell sees as the most immediate threat in *Nineteen Eighty-four*. Instead, a much more serious danger lies in totalitarianism, which, because it has fallen in love with power, has set itself against the realization of utopia. Indeed, as Orwell presents *Nineteen Eighty-four*, the totalitarian state is the greatest enemy of utopia, and one of its chief policies is to burn up the products of machine production in continuous warfare because "an all-round increase in wealth threatened the destruction—indeed, in some sense was the destruction—of a hierarchical society":

In a world in which everyone worked short hours, had enough to eat, lived in a house with a bathroom and a refrigerator, and possessed a motorcar or even an airplane, the most obvious and perhaps the most important form of inequality would already have disappeared. If it once became general, wealth would confer no distinction. It was possible, no doubt, to imagine a society in which *wealth*, in the sense of personal possessions and luxuries, should be evenly distributed, while *power* remained in the hands of a small privileged caste. But in practice such a society could not long remain stable. For if leisure and security were enjoyed by all alike, the great mass of human beings who are normally stupefied by poverty would become literate and would learn to think for themselves; and when once they had done this, they would sooner or later realize that the privileged minority had no function, and they would sweep it away. In the long run, a hierarchical society was only possible on a basis of poverty and ignorance. (1984 190–91)

And so, as the Book of Immanuel Goldstein explains, the world of 1984 has deliberately set itself against the realization of the "vision of a society unbelievably rich, leisured, orderly and efficient—a glittering antiseptic world of glass and steel and snow-white concrete" (p. 189). In the early twentieth century, says the Book, this vision was "part of the consciousness of nearly every literate person." From the very phrase itself—"glittering antiseptic world of glass and steel and snow-white concrete"—the world which the three great superstates of *Nineteen Eighty-four* have prevented from coming into existence must be the "Wells-world." Although Orwell had come to hate this Wellsian utopia, the nightmare of totalitarian power closing in on us was obviously a greater danger to human freedom and dignity.

And yet there is hidden in *Nineteen Eighty-four* considerable hostility to the machine. Thus, even though the rulers of Oceania have averted the utopia which machine civilization could bring, the monstrous world of 1984 could not exist without the machine, and in that nightmare world the machine serves only evil purposes: from telescreens to helicopters to the electric rack in the cellar of the Ministry of Love, it is used chiefly as an instrument of surveillance, propaganda, control, and torture. Orwell is saying that the machine makes a fully human life impossible.

In any case, it is not surprising that, although Orwell thought of Wells as a naïve prophet of mechanical progress, in writing *Nineteen Eighty-four* he was nevertheless greatly influenced by Wells. Orwell's nightmare utopia is, of course, especially indebted to *When the Sleeper Wakes*, as well as "A Story of the Days To Come" for plot, details, and images, but the character and extent of this indebtedness is complicated by the simultaneous influence of Zamyatin's *We*.

Orwell's article, "Freedom and Happiness," in which he pointed out the similarities between Huxley's *Brave New World* and Zamyatin's *We*, proves that Orwell knew Zamyatin's nightmare utopia very well indeed. And the parallels between *We* and *Nineteen Eighty-four* are astonishingly numerous.[25] Both portray a regimented society where individuality has been lost. Zamyatin's Well-Doer, Guardians, and devices for listening to the conversation of citizens are Orwell's Big Brother, Thought Police, and telescreens. Torture and confession, escape to nature, rebellion, love as a crime and political act are part of both books, while even the real coffee with real sugar which Winston and Julia drink in their hideout above Mr. Charrington's shop are paralleled by the cigarettes and alcohol in which D-503 and his mistress I-330 indulge. The endings, too, are remarkably similar. Winston, after treatment in the cellars of the Ministry of Love, comes to love O'Brien; and D-503, after undergoing the operation to remove the center of fancy, comes to believe once again that reason will prevail.

Obviously it would be very reasonable to assume that

these and other details in *Nineteen Eighty-four* come exclusively from *We*. But at best it could only be a partly accurate assumption, because Zamyatin in *We* was in turn enormously influenced by *When the Sleeper Wakes* and its companion, "A Story of the Days To Come," as his little book, *Herbert Wells*, proves. In addition, Orwell had carefully read these two stories by Wells.

Orwell very aptly summarized *When the Sleeper Wakes* with this sentence from *The Road to Wigan Pier*: "[Wells] draws a picture of a glittering, strangely sinister world in which the privileged class live a life of shallow gutless hedonism, and the workers, reduced to a state of utter slavery and sub-human ignorance, toil like troglodytes in caverns underground." [26] It is a summary which reveals what most interested Orwell in *When the Sleeper Wakes* and "A Story of the Days To Come"—that is, the picture of a slave state in a mechanical city. ("A Story of the Days To Come" also provided Orwell with basic elements of his plot. Elizabeth and Denton's romance set against the tyranny of the mechanical city is the prototype for the central dramatic action in *Nineteen Eighty-four*—Winston and Julia's secret love affair—as well as for all the similar affairs in numerous other anti-utopias, including that of D-503 and I-330 in *We*.)

Besides the central dramatic situation, numerous details and images can be traced back to *When the Sleeper Wakes* and "A Story of the Days To Come." Thus, for example, the "latter-day vile," beyond the reach of the phonograph culture of *When the Sleeper Wakes* and "A Story of the Days To Come," are without question Orwell's proles. Even Orwell's Thought Police are ultimately derived from a Wellsian detail—his Labour Police, armed with truncheons, too. Then the prototypes for the telescreens can be found in Wells's General Intelligence Machines, used to disseminate propaganda; the re-education of Winston Smith can be traced to the use of hypnotism in "A Story of the Days To Come," and so forth.

Finally, there are other details which, though not easily traced to a specific work, are nevertheless Wellsian. One of these is surely the novel-writing machine at which Julia works, another the memory holes down which unwanted documents are sent to be destroyed. Wellsian, too, is the great building which houses the Ministry of Truth: "an enormous pyramidal structure of glittering white concrete, soaring up, terrace after terrace, three hundred feet into the air" (p. 5). And Wellsian is "the place where there is no darkness":

> . . . a high ceilinged windowless cell with walls of glittering white porcelain. Concealed lamps flooded it with cold light, and there was a low, steady humming sound which he supposed had something to do with the air supply. (1984 229)

Even Newspeak, I think, at least suggests Wells. *Nineteen Eighty-four* is as greatly influenced by Wells as any of the anti-utopias we have so far discussed.

A full explanation of Orwell's indebtedness to *When the Sleeper Wakes* and its companion story must, however, take into consideration the ambivalence in his attitude toward these two stories. Orwell, as I have implied, thought highly of them as works of imagination. "The Story of the Days To Come" he called "splendid," and about *When the Sleeper Wakes*, which he contrasted with Wells's optimistic utopias, he wrote:

> But there is one Utopia book which stands in a rather different class from the others. This is "The Sleeper Wakes." In this book Wells drops all traces of optimism and forecasts a highly organized totalitarian society based quite frankly upon slave labour. In some ways it comes extremely close to what is actually happening, or appears to be happening, in the modern world, and it is in any case an astonishing feat of detailed imaginative construction.[27]

In fact, Orwell believed that, "considered merely as a piece of imaginative construction," *When the Sleeper Wakes* was "much superior" to Huxley's *Brave New World*. Both are very similar in that both forecast "a sort of prig's paradise in which all the dreams of the 'progressive' person come true." [28]

But although Orwell found *When the Sleeper Wakes* imaginatively superior to *Brave New World*, he believed the former "suffers from vast contradictions because of the fact that Wells, as the arch-priest of 'progress,' cannot write with any conviction *against* 'progress.'" And this contradiction is that in a machine-world like that imagined by Wells in *When the Sleeper Wakes*, "the workers might be enslaved, ill-treated, and even underfed, but they certainly would not be condemned to ceaseless manual toil; because in that case what would be the function of the machine?" Actually, said Orwell, Wells was only trying to suggest that progress "might take a wrong turning," and so Wells limited himself to imagining only one evil: "inequality—one class grabbing all the wealth and power and oppressing the others, apparently out of pure spite." [29] According to Orwell, what Wells is really trying to say is that if we overthrew capitalism and replaced it with socialism, then machine civilization would be fine. In effect Orwell took *When the Sleeper Wakes*, as well as "A Story of the Days To Come," and used it for another purpose, and, by imagining perpetual war to consume the surplus of machine production, he eliminated the contradiction into which he thought Wells had fallen.

I N "THE MACHINE STOPS," *We, Brave New World,* and *Nineteen Eighty-four,* we observe an anti-utopia which, though differing in numerous features, is much the same each time it has appeared. In C. S. Lewis's trilogy— *Out of the Silent Planet* (1938), *Perelandra* (1943), *That Hideous Strength* (1945)—anti-utopia assumes a new and different appearance. One reason for this change is, of course, that instead of being a reaction to utopia from a "disillusioned left," the trilogy is an attack from a conservative, Christian right. At the same time the trilogy is a kind of *Paradise Lost* employed to teach Christian doctrine to a sophisticated but unsuspecting twentieth century, and thus, more than any other anti-utopia, it generates an enveloping myth. If in *Brave New World* and *Nineteen Eighty-four* we saw Wellsian science fiction moving further from myth to satire, in Lewis's trilogy we find it returning very much to myth again. Yet the trilogy, though anti-Wellsian, owes as heavy a debt to Wells as any of the anti-utopias we have discussed, a debt which is especially natural in view of Lewis's strong and genuine interest in science fiction, including the pulp variety. (Besides the trilogy, his interest manifested itself in three excellent stories, two of them written for *The Magazine of Fantasy and Science Fiction*; an essay, "On Science Fiction," originally read to the English Club at Cambridge; and a discussion held with Kingsley Amis for the first issue of *SF Horizons*.[1])

The very Wellsian idea of travel to other worlds provides the chief myth of the trilogy. According to Lewis's conception, the earth, the only fallen world of all the inhabited ones in the universe and an enemy-occupied territory in the civil war between Heaven and Satan, has been quarantined to prevent the spread of its spiritual infection. So the rest of the universe had heard nothing from earth (called Thulcandra—the silent planet), since the great war, when earth's Bent One (Satan) was driven back out of the heavens and bound in the air of his own world. Then the opportunist-adventurer Devine and the physicist Weston break the barrier by journeying to Malacandra—Mars—in a space ship. "By enginry and natural philosophy," these two men inadvertently begin a new chapter in the history of the universe, and in so doing pull down "Deep Heaven" on the heads of themselves and others who work for the Bent One, the Black Archon of Thulcandra.

The trilogy begins, then, in *Out of the Silent Planet*, when Weston and Devine, mistakenly believing a sacrificial offering is necessary, kidnap the Cambridge philologist, Ransom, and make a second journey to Malacandra. A good deal of the imaginative richness derives from Wells's *The First Men in the Moon*, which Lewis praised as "the best of the sort I have ever read." [2] The steel globe with shutters in which Ransom travels is Bedford and Cavor's sphere; many of the details of the journey, such as the constant tinkling of meteorites on the steel shell of the ship and the pulsing vitality of space, come from Wells's lunar voyage; and the riot of vegetation on Malacandra is inspired by Wells's marvelous imaginings of the rapid growth of vegetation in craters at the dawn of a lunar day.

The climax of the book comes in an interview with the Oyarsa, the ruling spirit of Malacandra, which is not only reminiscent of Gulliver's audience with the King of Brobdingnag but even more of its descendant, Cavor's audience with the Grand Lunar. In this scene Weston—he and Devine have been captured after killing three of the inhabitants of Malacandra—extols the superiority of earthly to Malacandrian civilization. Weston, a man who believes that the human species must spread itself throughout the universe, insists upon man's right to supersede the Malacandrians as the right of the higher over the lower. "Your tribal life, with its stone-age weapons and bee-hive huts, its primitive coracles and elementary social structure," he tells the Oyarsa, "has nothing to compare with our civilization with our science, medicine and law, our armies, our architecture, our commerce, and our transport system which is rapidly annihilating space and time" (p. 146). Just how superior this civilization really is Lewis made clear by the technique of having Ransom attempt to translate Weston's speech— Weston speaks Malacandrian very badly—for the Oyarsa. Translated into the language of an unfallen world, Weston's praise of earthly science, medicine and law, armies, architecture, commerce, and transportation sounds like this:

He [Weston] says we know much. There is a thing happens in our world when the body of a living creature feels pain and becomes weak, and he says we sometimes know how to stop it. He says we have many bent [Malacandrian for criminal] people and we kill them or shut them in huts and that we have people for settling quarrels between the bent *hnau* about their huts and mates and things. He says we have many ways for the *hnau* of one land to kill those of another and some are trained to it. He says we build very big and strong huts of stone and other things—like the pfifltriggi [a frog-like people who are the artisans of Malacandra]. And he says we exchange many things among ourselves and carry heavy weights very quickly a long way. Because of all this, he says it would not be the act of a bent *hnau* if our people killed all your people. (*OSP* 147)

The Malacandrians are warned, and the Oyarsa sends the steel sphere back to earth, "unbodying" it shortly after its arrival in an incident that more than reminds us of the disappearance of the Cavorite sphere immediately upon Bedford's return.

The second volume, *Perelandra*, though a journey to Venus—Perelandra—is much less Wellsian. There are, of course, a few touches suggestive of Wells. The alien vegetation on the floating islands perhaps owes something in its lushness to Wells's lunar vegetation; Weston arrives again in Bedford and Cavor's sphere; and certain hints of the rational insect life inside the Perelandrian mountain echo Wells's Selenites. But chiefly *Perelandra* is a theological fantasy, in which Ransom, transported to Perelandra by the Oyarsa, defeats the Un-Man who, having possessed the body of Weston, is trying to tempt Tinidril, the Eve of Perelandra, into disobedience of God's command. Man on Perelandra thus does not fall.

The adventures which began with Ransom's journey to Malacandra culminate in *That Hideous Strength*, the most anti-utopian volume in the trilogy and the one in which Wells appears in person as Horace Jules, the figurehead director of the National Institute for Co-ordinated Experiments. In *That Hideous Strength* the dark spirits of earth inspire evil men, those who actually lead the N.I.C.E., to work to turn the world into a nightmare society where behavior is scientifically manipulated. The N.I.C.E. is a fictional embodiment of Lewis's fears about a new science of man which are set forth more directly in his little book, *The Abolition of Man* (1943). In that book Lewis argued that the traditional system of values will inevitably be destroyed by such a science of human nature—that when man has seen through human nature there will be nothing to guide him except the lowest kind of animal impulses. And then, in this moral vacuum, the world will consist of the great mass of men—the conditioned—snug and unknowing under the rule of the behavioral scientists, the conditioners. It is this situation which the N.I.C.E.—backed by the powers of Thulcandra—tries to create on earth. The savagery of Lewis's attack can be seen in the remarks of one of the members of the N.I.C.E. about the purposes of the Institute:

"Man has got to take charge of Man. That means, remember, that some men have got to take charge of the rest. . . ."

"What sort of thing have you in mind?"

"Quite simple and obvious things, at first—sterilization of the unfit, liquidation of backward races (we don't want any dead weights), selective breeding. Then real education, including pre-natal education. By real education I mean one that has no 'take-it-or-leave-it' nonsense. A real education makes the patient what it wants infallibly: whatever he or his parents try to do about it. Of course, it'll have to be mainly psychological at first. But we'll get on to biochemical conditioning in the end and direct manipulation of the brain. . . ." (*HS* 37)

But fortunately the realization of this utopia is prevented. The opposition to the N.I.C.E. is headed by Ransom and a little company of Christians, supported by the Oyarsa of each planet, the great *eldila* ("spirits" or "angels" would be our closest approximation) of the solar system who can now enter the sphere of the earth because Weston and Devine have destroyed the barrier that had previously kept Thulcandra quarantined. Ransom, who turns out to be Mr. Fisher-King as well as the current Pendragon of Logres (King of Arthur's realm, which continues to exist in secrecy), is also assisted by a clairvoyant young woman, by a bear, and by the Arthurian Merlin, who has awakened from his centuries-long trance to play a crucial role at this crisis in history. In its use of Arthurian myth to provide meaning, *That Hideous Strength* can, of course, be profitably studied in connection with T. S. Eliot's *Wasteland* and such poems by Charles Williams as *The Figure of Arthur* and *Taliessin Through Logres.* (The best study of this sort is Charles Moorman's *Arthurian Triptych.*[3])

The climax of *That Hideous Strength* comes in the great banquet scene at Belbury when H. G. Wells, alias Horace Jules, delivers a talk to the assembled dignitaries of the N.I.C.E. The scene also climaxes the caricature of Jules, who has been presented on and off throughout the novel as a conceited and dangerous fool who does not realize where the science he champions is taking mankind. Without any actual power, Jules is, of course, regarded with contempt by the working members of the Institute:

"Jules! Hell's bells!" said Feverstone. "You don't imagine that little mascot has anything to say to what really goes on? He's all right for selling the Institute to the great British public in the Sunday papers and he draws a whacking salary. He's no use for work. There's nothing inside his head except some nineteenth-century socialist stuff, and blah about the rights of man. He's just about got as far as Darwin." (*HS* 39)

What to do with him when he makes a visit is really quite a problem for the people of the Institute:

Conversation with Mr. Jules was always difficult because he insisted on regarding himself not as a figurehead but as the real director of the Institute, and even as the source of most of its ideas. And since, in fact, any science he knew was that taught him at the University of London over fifty years ago, and any philosophy he knew had been acquired from writers like Haeckel and Joseph McCabe and Winwood Reade, it was not, in fact, possible to talk to him about most of the things the Institute was really doing. One was always engaged in inventing answers to the questions which were actually meaningless and expressing enthusiasm for ideas which were out of date and had been crude even in their prime. (*HS* 401–2)

At times Lewis's attack takes on a personal coloring, as when he describes Jules as a cockney, "a very little man, whose legs were so short that he had unkindly been compared with a duck." Years of good living and conceit, says Lewis, had interfered with a certain original *bonhomie*.

At first, as Jules delivers his after-dinner speech, the diners seem undisturbed in their digestive contentment and the pursuit of their own thoughts. Then gradually the audience grows dangerously quiet as the double-talk that Jules is spouting penetrates their consciousness:

To different members of the audience the change came differently. To Frost it began at the moment when he heard Jules end a sentence with the words, "as gross an anachronism as to trust to Calvary for salvation in modern war." *Cavalry*, thought Frost almost aloud. Why couldn't the fool mind what he was saying? The blunder irritated him extremely. Perhaps—but hullo! what was this? Had his hearing gone wrong? For Jules seemed to be saying that the future density of mankind depended on the implosion of the horses of Nature. "He's drunk," thought Frost. Then, crystal clear in articulation beyond all possibility of mistake, came, "The madrigore of verjuice must be talthibianised." (*HS* 409)

The speech in time leads to riot and chaos, in which Jules and the others are killed. All of this has been brought about by the power of Deep Heaven working through Merlin. At the end the Institute and its artifacts are destroyed by fire and earthquake, and so for a time the danger to mankind is ended, the nightmare utopia does not come into existence.

II

But Lewis's anti-Wellsianism in the trilogy is deeper, much more complicated and more extensive than is evident even in the caricature drawn in Horace Jules. This anti-Wellsianism is, of course, congruent with his attack on the secularism and scientific materialism that he sees as the greatest enemy of Christianity in the twentieth century. The inception of the trilogy as an anti-utopian attack using the myth of space travel is explained in a passage from a letter written by Lewis and quoted by Roger Lancelyn Green:

> What immediately spurred me to write . . . was Olaf Stapledon's *Last and First Men* and an essay in J. B. S. Haldane's *Possible Worlds*, both of which seemed to take the idea of such [Space] travel seriously and to have the desperately immoral outlook which I try to pillory in Weston. I liked the whole interplanetary idea as *mythology* and simply wished to conquer for my own (Christian) point of view what has hitherto been used by the opposite side. I think Wells's *First Men in the Moon* the best of the sort I have ever read. . . .[4]

What the opposite side is up to is clearly evident in *Last and First Men* and in two essays from *Possible Worlds*, "Man's Destiny" and "Last Judgment."[5] There Stapledon and Haldane present a "ghastly materialistic" philosophy that there is no heaven or hell and when a man dies he is gone forever; and that the only hope man has of improving his lot is through the application of the human mind—that is, through science. Both works see man so applying his mind, thereby controlling evolution and eventually colonizing other planets. Thus *Last and First Men*—Stapledon's masterpiece and the most favorably received of his work—

traces the future history of man through eighteen species, including a migration to Venus and then to Neptune as changing conditions in the solar system require. At the end, man cannot escape destruction, but—as Lewis's student, Roger Lancelyn Green, described it, surely echoing Lewis's feelings—Stapledon "leaves them still rejoicing in their hideous pride and the 'task of seminating among the stars the seeds of a new humanity.' " [6] Stapledon's Last Men in their "arrogance" conclude that "It was good to have been man."

The same values are present in Haldane's two essays. Civilization, he wrote in "Man's Destiny," is a poor thing, and our only hope of improvement is in science. Particularly man must learn to control his evolution, and to this, Haldane feared, there will be opposition, most likely from organized religion:

If science is to improve man as it has improved his environment, the experimental method must be applied to him. It is quite likely that the attempt to do so will rouse such fierce opposition that science will again be persecuted as it has been in the past. Such a persecution may quite well be successful, especially if it is supported by religion. A world-wide religious revival, whether Christian or not, would probably succeed in suppressing experimental inquiry into the human mind, which offers the only serious hope of improving it.[7]

This strangling of scientific research before mankind has learned to control its own evolution was, for Haldane, a very strong possibility, in which case mankind will go down to darkness and oblivion. (In 1946 in "Auld Hornie, F.R.S.," Haldane attacked Lewis's trilogy for just this opposition to science.[8])

But if man does learn to control his evolution, then "there will be no limit to man's material, intellectual, and spiritual progress" (in their essential features Haldane's exceptional men of the future are Stapledon's Last Men):

Less than a million years hence the average man or woman will realize all the possibilities that human life has so far shown. He or she will never know a minute's illness. He will be able to think like Newton, to write like Racine, to paint like Fra Angelica, to compose like Bach. He will be as incapable of hatred as St. Francis, and when death comes at the end of a life probably measured in thousands of years he will meet it with as little fear as Captain Oates or Arnold von Winkelreid. And every minute of his life will be lived with all the passion of a lover or a discoverer. We can form no idea whatever of the exceptional men of such a future.[9]

And then, of course, men will voyage interstellar space and colonize other planets.

The values inherent in Haldane's utopianism are even more explicit in "Last Judgment," which Lewis in his talk on science fiction at Cambridge called brilliant but depraved. Haldane's essay imagines a distant future when a small group of our descendants migrate to Venus to preserve the human species after the earth is destroyed by the fall of the moon. On the new planet the colonists realize that man's destiny is "eternity and infinity," and they adopt an ethic in which the future of the species is more important than anything else. Lewis expressed his horror not only in the trilogy but in other writings, most notably in the posthumously published "A Reply to Professor Haldane," which, though inspired by Haldane's "Auld Hornie, F.R.S.," refers to "Last Judgment." Lewis's definition of "scientism" in the "Reply" explains his opinion of the values of Haldane's men of the future: "It is, in a word, the belief that the supreme end is the perpetuation of our own species, and this is to be pursued even if, in the process of being fitted for survival, our species has to be stripped of all those things for which we value it—of pity, of happiness, and of freedom."[10]

Obviously Stapledon's and Haldane's future men are identical with Wells's Men Like Gods. Nor can there be any question that Stapledon and Haldane in their utopianism were powerfully influenced by Wells. In a letter to Wells dated October 16, 1931, Stapledon explained why he had not acknowledged his indebtedness to Wells in writing *Last and First Men:* "A man does not record his debt to the air he breathes." [11] Similarly, although Haldane was a Marxist and often disagreed with Wells, still he referred to him frequently in his writings and admitted that the very mention of the future suggested him. So in attacking Stapledon and Haldane, Lewis was also in a very real sense attacking Wells.[12]

All of these Wells-Stapledon-Haldane ideas are directly embodied in the trilogy. Thus in the first volume Lewis made the scientist, Weston, the chief villain (Lewis might well have Haldane personally in mind here) and had him give the following explanation of why he has come to Malacandra:

"She [Life] has ruthlessly broken down all obstacles and liquidated all failures and to-day in her highest form—civilized man—and in me as his representative, she presses forward to that interplanetary leap which will, perhaps, place her for ever beyond the reach of death."

. . . .

"It is in her right," said Weston, "the right, or, if you will, the might of Life herself, that I am prepared without flinching to plant the flag of man on the soil of Malacandra: to march on, step by step, superseding, where necessary, the lower forms of life that we find, claiming planet after planet, system after system, till our posterity—whatever strange form and yet unguessed mentality they have assumed—dwell in the universe wherever the universe is habitable." (*OSP* 148)

In *Perelandra* this characterization of Weston is continued; he is described as a man obsessed with the "idea that humanity, having now sufficiently corrupted the planet where it arose, must at all costs contrive to seed itself over a larger area. . . ." (p. 80) Lewis's hatred of Weston, of course, reaches a peak when it is revealed that he allowed his body to be the vehicle by which the Bent One comes to Perelandra to re-enact the temptation in the Garden of Eden.

In *That Hideous Strength*, Lewis's hostility to the Wells-Stapledon-Haldane ideas became even more overt; there he showed what he believed would happen if these ideas were put into effect. While to the public the N.I.C.E. may seem no more than an attempt to have "science applied to social problems and backed by the whole force of the state," ultimately it hopes to take over the human race, recondition it, control evolution, and finally make "man a really efficient animal"—in other words, bring about the situation of humanity being snug under the conditioners which Lewis foresaw in *The Abolition of Man*. In the context of the novel all this means cutting man away from the animal, turning him into a species of giant brains, something like Stapledon's giant brains or Wells's Martians, and destroying as much of the organic life of the planet as possible, a process of cleansing that Wells himself occasionally seemed to encourage. "It is," one of the leaders of the N.I.C.E. says, "the beginning of Man Immortal and Man Ubiquitous . . . Man on the throne of the universe" (pp. 203–4). Or as another character explains,

It is to bring out of that cocoon of organic life which sheltered the babyhood of mind the New Man, the man who will not die, the artificial man, free from Nature. Nature is the ladder we have climbed up by, now we kick her away. (*HS* 202)

By showing the dark *eldila* of earth as aiding the men of the N.I.C.E. so to create the New Man, Lewis presented a grotesque and sinister caricature of the vision so often identified with Wells. No anti-utopia exists which is more counter-Wellsian than *That Hideous Strength*.

CHAPTER VIII

WHILE THE anti-utopian tradition was establishing
itself during the early decades of this century, other
works than those we have so far discussed were being written
with a more or less strong infusion of anti-utopian values.
Among these are G. K. Chesterton's *The Napoleon of Not-
ting Hill* (1904), R. H. Benson's *Lord of the World* (1907),
Rose Macaulay's *What Not* (1918), A.E.'s *The Interpreters*
(1922), Charlotte Haldane's *Man's World* (1926), as well
as many of the other, generally trivial "tales of the future"
listed in I. F. Clarke's bibliography and Everett F. Bleiler's
Checklist of Fantastic Literature.[1] Most of these works are
also anti-Wellsian. The excellent but little-known *The Interpreters*, for example, tells of a night of revolt against a

Wellsian scientific state, during which five imprisoned intellectuals discuss the philosophical and ethical justification for the rebellion. But none of these books, not even A.E.'s, represent the anti-utopian tradition full-blown, and none have much influence on that tradition.[2] It is the kind of antiutopia we have been discussing, whose form must have been forever and spectacularly set with the publication of *Brave New World* in 1932, which constitutes the tradition.[3]

In the late 1930's the only anti-utopia at all outstanding is Ayn Rand's *Anthem* (1938). It describes a World State a thousand years in the future when the "We" of collectivism has replaced the "I" of individualism. Many of its details seem to derive from Zamyatin's *We*, which Miss Rand may have read before she left Russia in 1925. Citizens have numbers instead of names and lead carefully regimented lives, living in bare white barracks and eating in communal dining halls. The sexual act is permitted only in spring with partners chosen by the state; children are raised in state nurseries and schools.

The hero, Equality 7-2521, is a gifted individual, unable to suppress his genius, who escapes, after torture and imprisonment, into the great Uncharted Forest with the golden-haired Liberty 5-3000. Over the door of the glass house of the ancients, to which the couple finally journey, he carves the word "Ego" (reminiscent of the "Mephi" of Zamyatin's rebels). The curious thing about this book, however, is the nature of its anti-Wellsianism. It is anti-Wellsian in its opposition to the collective state, but at the same time it admires what other anti-utopians dislike: science and technology. (One of the evils of the collective state is that it has allowed civilization to slip back to a pre-industrial level.) Two decades later Miss Rand rewrote it in a second and much less successful anti-utopia, *Atlas Shrugged* (1957). The latter—a wordy, digressive, 1168-page polemic—is so filled with hate and offers a creed so much the negation of humane values that it is hard to imagine even the anti-utopians most opposed to collectivism as able to accept its worship of selfishness. Forster, Zamyatin, Huxley, Orwell, after all, rejected utopia for what they thought was the good of mankind.

After World War II the tradition which produced *Anthem* broke loose with an incredible flood of books describing regimented nightmare states. Although these postwar anti-utopias, with the exception of *Nineteen Eighty-four*, are seldom if ever consciously related to Wells, they still contain strong Wellsian (or anti-Wellsian) elements, probably embedded in the form itself as it was borrowed from *Nineteen Eighty-four* or earlier major anti-utopias. In general the minor anti-utopias of the postwar period, which are now briefly our concern, fall into two broad categories, those written by what might be loosely called "mainstream" writers and those by "professional" science-fiction writers. Oddly enough, the vitality of the original anti-utopias is best preserved in the works by "professional" science-fiction writers. It should be remembered, of course, that works by writers in both categories must, according to our definition in Chapter I, be considered "science fiction." And it should also be noted that since the rise of Hitler and Stalin there have been a few novels which portray, under the guise of fiction, existing totalitarian states. Two of these, Arthur Koestler's *Darkness at Noon* (1941) and Vladimir Nabokov's *Bend Sinister* (1947), are very good indeed, but they should not be confused with the Wellsian kind of anti-utopia we have been considering. They do not extrapolate; they are not science fiction in the manner of *Nineteen Eighty-four*, even with all its allusions to Stalinist Russia.

Besides *Nineteen Eighty-four*, there are about six "mainstream" Wellsian anti-utopias of some importance in the period since World War II, but none have the impact of Orwell's. All are minor and often flawed in various ways. David Karp's *One* (1953), which narrates the brainwashing of a gifted professor by a mediocrity-enforcing state, dissipates much of its effectiveness by being too openly an expression of academic paranoia. Franz Werfel's *Star of the Unborn* (1946), a tale of a distant future when men live underground in effete refinement, is too long and slow-moving to be altogether successful. Gore Vidal's *Messiah* (1953) tells how an ex-undertaker with a hypnotic personality founds a religion of death that, promoted by the techniques of modern publicity, sweeps the world to become a tyranny. It is, as one reviewer remarked, ingenious rather than profound.

The other three "mainstream" anti-utopias are more felicitous. Evelyn Waugh's *Love Among the Ruins* (1953), though only *"a little jeu d'esprit,"* is at times brilliantly satiric. It describes a dingy Welfare State where Remedial Treatment has replaced punishment and no man is "held responsible for his own acts." While it echoes both *Brave New World* and *Nineteen Eighty-four* (in such features as greetings like "State be with you" and in the drabness of its world), it lacks both the inventiveness and the concentration of detail that contribute to the more powerful effect of the works by Huxley and Orwell.

Longer and more sustained is Anthony Burgess's *A Clockwork Orange* (1962), another fantasy of a drab socialist England of the future, this time one in which teenage gangs, speaking a slang derived from Russian, terrorize London. The story is told by its anti-hero, a fifteen-year-old hoodlum named Alex, who leads his gang through the nighttime streets, raping young women and bashing older citizens in the eyes with bicycle chains. Eventually Alex is caught and sentenced to prison for murder, but the authorities decide to rehabilitate and release him. He is conditioned by "Ludovico's Technique" to commit only socially acceptable acts, becomes "a little machine capable only of good." (The State hopes to clear its prisons of criminals to make room for political offenders.) On his release from prison, Alex falls in the hands of an opposition party, which attempts to use his loss of moral choice to bring down the government in the next election. But the government counters by de-conditioning him and jailing its opponents, and it wins the election.

The dinginess of the world of *A Clockwork Orange* again suggests *Nineteen Eighty-four*, while the use of conditioning seems derivative from *Brave New World*, but the book has a quality of its own, chiefly because of Burgess's lovingly inventive use of language. (Altogether it is considerably more effective than Burgess's other anti-utopia, the sadly incoherent *The Wanting Seed* [1963], which describes a future rationalist state in which men are vegetarian and homosexuality is encouraged to control population. After a sudden blight and resulting famine the rationalist state gives way to cannibalism, sex orgies, and wars contrived to limit population again.)

The most richly conceived and the most profound in meaning of the postwar "mainstream" anti-utopias is L. P. Hartley's *Facial Justice* (1960), a work highly pleasing in that its style succeeds in projecting a believable world of the future, despite occasional inconsistencies in details. The best of its kind, it deserves a more extended discussion to show how the Wellsian anti-utopia fares in the 1960's.

Facial Justice exhibits, beneath its ingenious variations, the familiar features of the counter-Wellsian anti-utopia. "In the not very distant future, after the Third World War," men have emerged from underground to take up life again on the surface. The destruction has been incredible. Not only have nine-tenths of the human race been destroyed, but the very topography and climate have been changed. In England, where the story is set, atomic weapons have "stripped the countryside of verdure, replacing green with a color like mud but colder, grayer, and less luminous." In many places, war has leveled the hills and filled up the valleys. And the weather is perpetual March: "an east wind blew, and gray clouds, which the sun never quite got through, though its position was visible behind them, scudded across the sky."

A benevolent dictator ("Darling Dictator") rules with the help of the Inspectors, the familiar utopian elite, over the new civilization which comes to flourish in this gray flat land which was once England. It is a "relaxed and invalidish civilization," with everything suggestive of "weakness and convalescence." The people are called Patients and Delinquents by the Dictator, who systematically lowers their vitality by making them take daily doses of bromide. To remind them of their fallen condition, each is given the name of a murderer (to which name is added a number in the manner of *We*). The Horizontal View of Life prevails. The greatest evil is envy, the greatest good is equality. And so women undergo plastic surgery to give them standardized Beta faces which, though they produce desire in men, will not arouse envy. Even the buildings reflect this way of life: "a sort of toadstool architecture" in which circles and curves predominate, sharp corners are used sparingly, and nothing rises higher than two stories.

Behind all this can be detected the outline of the usual inverted utopia written in reaction to Wells: the cataclysmic war which precedes the new state, the rule of the omniscient dictator, the guardian elite, the standardization of men and women, including artificial faces and numbers for names, the substitution of the manufactured (plastic flowers and trees) for the natural, and the familiar revolt against the regime.

But then there is something different about this latter-day anti-utopia. The new quality was aptly caught by the reviewer in the *Times Literary Supplement* when, contrasting *Facial Justice* with *Nineteen Eighty-four*, he described the world of *Facial Justice* as "more pathetic than horrific" and its narration as having "the odd contrived remoteness of a dream rather than the inevitability of a nightmare." [4] As with the other minor works we have just discussed, the force of the anti-utopian tradition has virtually spent itself.

II

A much more vigorous recent manifestation of the anti-utopian tradition occurred in the 1950's, when it filtered down to a popular level and appeared in pulp science fiction. Much of the unusual vitality of the anti-utopias by "professional" science-fiction writers derives from the medium itself, which, though Wellsian in its origins, is very largely an American phenomenon, unlike the anti-utopias which have been the chief subject of this book.

So established in popular usage has the term "science fiction" become that *Webster's Third* and *Webster's Seventh New Collegiate* include a definition of it: "fiction dealing principally with the impact of actual or imagined science upon society or individuals." This, we need hardly point out, is broad enough to cover everything we have discussed in this book, from *The Time Machine* to *Facial Justice*. In the beginning, however, "science fiction," or, as it was first called, "scientifiction," was exclusively a publishing category, referring to crude novels or short stories of this type published in cheap editions or, most often, in pulp magazines, which we have suggested partly explains the unfavorable connotations the term has for so many educated people. But gradually during the 1930's the quality of this fiction began to improve, and the process continued until in the postwar era the level of talent writing for the pulp magazines was surprisingly high, often high enough for a work of real literature to be produced, albeit a minor one. Thus it was that science fiction attracted the attention of at least a few intellectuals sensitive to literary values, as it did in Kingsley Amis's pioneer study, *New Maps of Hell*. An even more eloquent testimony to its merit was provided in the five *Spectrum* anthologies edited by Kingsley Amis and Robert Conquest. From our point of view, the most important aspect of this phenomenon was the development of an anti-utopian strain.

Up to the 1950's, science fiction had been permeated with the Wellsian vision, which is not surprising since Wells was a kind of patron saint for the early science-fiction writers. Indeed, Hugo Gernsback helped fill out many issues of the first pulp science-fiction magazine, *Amazing Stories*, by reprinting Wells's stories. Often the Wellsian vision is watered down to the single idea that science and technology, by extending man's power to the performance of all things possible, will inevitably improve the human condition, an over-simplified view Wells himself never took. But stated or implied, this unthinking optimism about the effect of science and technology on human life has been the animating spirit of much science fiction. It is even implicit in the poorest class of science fiction—space opera—works which are descended from Edgar Rice Burroughs's *A Princess of Mars* and which are little more than Rider Haggard adventure transferred to space, works in which science is simply equated with magic. It is also implicit in the more sophisticated stories (beautifully discussed by the late Basil Davenport [5]) which, characterized by exuberance of imagination, improvise on the consequences of real or imagined inventions or scientific discoveries. Good examples of this kind of science fiction are novels and stories like A. J. Deutsch's "A Subway Named Moebius" (1950), which plays with the idea of a subway system constructed in the form of a Moebius band, whose passengers disappear for ten weeks into the fourth dimension; Hal Clement's *Mission of Gravity* (1953), which carefully pieces together the ecology of the dense planet circling 61 Cygni; and J. G. Ballard's "The Voices of Time" (1960), which deals with the increasing manifestations of a universe running down, from countdown signals from the galaxies to the wearing out of the ribonucleic acid templates which unravel the protein chains in all living organisms. Writers of this class of science fiction have clearly in mind the assumptions that man can master the principles of this cause-and-effect universe and that such mastery will necessarily better the human lot.

Occasionally the Wellsian utopian vision has been stated directly in science fiction, as it has in Arthur Clarke's near classic, *Childhood's End* (1953), a book which is still in print after fourteen years. Apparently indebted to Kurd Lasswitz's utopian romance, *Auf Zwei Planeten* (1897), as well as to Wells's histories of the future, *The World Set Free* and *The Shape of Things To Come, Childhood's End* describes the bloodless conquest of earth by the Overlords, vastly superior creatures who come to our world in order to prepare the human race for its next stage of development, an eventual merging with the composite mind of the universe. Arriving just in time to stop men from turning their planet into a radioactive wasteland, the Overlords unite earth into one world, in which justice, order, and benevolence prevail and ignorance, poverty, and fear have ceased to exist. Under their rule, earth becomes a technological utopia. Both abolition of war and new techniques of production, particularly robot factories, greatly increase the world's wealth, a situation described in the following passage, which has the true utopian ring:

Everything was so cheap that the necessities of life were free, provided as a public service by the community, as roads, water, street lighting and drainage had once been. A man could travel anywhere he pleased, eat whatever he fancied—without handing over any money.[6]

With destructive tensions and pressures removed, men have the vigor and energy to construct a new human life—rebuilding entire cities, expanding facilities for entertainment, providing unlimited opportunities for education—indeed, for the first time giving everyone the chance to employ his talents to the fullest. Mankind, as a result, attains previously undreamed of levels of civilization and culture, a golden age which the Overlords, a very evident symbol of science, have helped produce by introducing reason and the scientific method into human activities. In the Wellsian manner, science is the savior of mankind.

What is remarkable then is that during the 1950's science-fiction writers turned about and attacked their own cherished vision of the future—attacked the *Childhood's End* kind of faith. And they did this on a very large scale, with a veritable flood of novels and stories which are either anti-utopias or narratives of adventure with anti-utopian elements. Because of the means of publication—science-fiction magazines and cheap paperbacks—the full range and extent of this phenomenon is difficult to assess, though one fact is evident: the science-fiction imagination has been immensely fertile in its extrapolations. Among the anti-utopias, for example, Isaac Asimov's *The Caves of Steel* (1954) portrays the deadly effects on human life of the super-city of the future; James Blish's *A Case of Conscience* (1958) describes a world hiding from its own weapons of destruction in underground shelters; Frederik Pohl's "The Midas Touch" (1954) predicts an economy of abundance which, in order to remain prosperous, must set its robots to consuming surplus production; Clifford D. Simak's "How-2" (1954) tells of a future when robots have taken over, leaving men with nothing to do; and Robert Sheckley's *The Status Civilization* (1960) describes a world which, frightened by the powers of destruction science has given it, becomes static and conformist. And then there are the three science-fiction anti-utopias which achieve the greatest significance as literature, Frederik Pohl and C. M. Kornbluth's *The Space Merchants* (1953), Kurt Vonnegut, Jr.'s *Player Piano* (1952), and Ray Bradbury's *Fahrenheit 451* (1954), works which we will later examine in detail. The novels and stories like Pohl's *Drunkard's Walk* (1960), with the focus on adventure and with the anti-utopian elements only a dim background—in this case an uneasy, overpopulated world in which the mass of people do uninteresting routine jobs while a carefully selected, university-trained elite runs everything—are in all likelihood as numerous as the anti-utopias.

There is no single explanation of why so many science-fiction writers began writing counter-Wellsian anti-utopias. The enormous impact of *Nineteen Eighty-four* in 1949 surely inspired many science-fiction writers to produce warnings of nightmare futures. But this can hardly be the only reason, for science-fiction anti-utopias occasionally appeared before 1949, such as Jack Williamson's "With Folded Hands" (1949), the classic story of men replaced by their own robots. The anti-utopian movement among science-fiction writers must also have responded to the change in popular attitudes which was the result of a filtering down of the earlier anti-utopianism of intellectuals plus a growing public awareness of the dangers of scientifically planned collectivism as these had been pointed up by Nazi Germany and Stalinist Russia. (The broadly based readership for *Nineteen Eighty-four* is excellent evidence of this shift in attitudes.) Finally, science-fiction writers—usually highly intelligent—knew *Brave New World*, which they often regarded with pride as science fiction that had won acceptance from the literary "mainstream." In any case, the Wellsian influence is still present in the science-fiction anti-utopias, and it is sometimes very great, as can be seen in *The Space Merchants, Fahrenheit 451*, and *Player Piano*.

Probably the least known of these three novels is *The Space Merchants*, a good example of a science-fiction anti-utopia which extrapolates much more than the impact of science on human life (though its most important warning is in this area, namely the use to which discoveries in the behavioral sciences may be put). The novel is a Wellsian fantasy, set in the future with all kinds of technological marvels, but the scheme of the Wellsian utopia is greatly attentuated. About all that is obviously left of that scheme is the idea of a ruling elite, the one-sixteenth of the population who run the advertising agencies and big corporations which control the rest of the people, the submerged fifteen-sixteenths who are the workers and consumers, with the government being no more than "a clearing house for pressures." At times the novel is brilliantly satiric of our way of life. Like ours, the economy of the space merchants must constantly expand in order to survive, and, like ours, it is based on the principle of "ever increasing everybody's work and profits in the circle of consumption." The consequences, of course, have been dreadful: reckless expansion has led to overpopulation, pollution of the earth and depletion of its natural resources. For example, even the most successful executive lives in a two-room apartment—ordinary people rent space in the stairwells of office buildings, where they sleep at night; soyaburgers have replaced meat, and wood has become so precious that it is saved for expensive jewelry; and the atmosphere is so befouled that no one dares walk in the open without respirators or soot plugs.

But the deepest criticism offered by *The Space Merchants* is its warning against the dangers inherent in perfecting "a science of man and his motives," and in this respect the book takes on something of the anti-Wellsian coloration of *Brave New World.* Pohl and Kornbluth's ad men have long since thrown out appeals to reason, and have developed techniques of advertising which tie in with "every basic trauma and neurosis in American life," which work on the libido of consumers, which are linked to the "great prime motivations of the human spirit." As the hero, Mitchell Courtenay, explains before his conversion, the job of advertising is "to convince people without letting them know that they're being convinced." And to do this requires first of all the kind of information about people which is provided by the scientists in industrial anthropology and consumer research, who, for example, tell Courtenay that three days is the "optimum priming period for a closed social circuit to be triggered with a catalytic cue-phrase"—which means that an effective propaganda technique is to send an idea into circulation and then three days later reinforce or undermine it. And the second requirement for convincing people without their knowledge is the artistic talent to persuade by using principles which the scientists have discovered. Thus the copy-writer in the world of the space merchants is the person who in earlier ages might have been a lyric poet, the person "capable of putting together words that stir and move and sing." As Courtenay explains, "Here in this profession we reach into the souls of men and women. And we do it by taking talent—and redirecting it."

Now the basic question to be asked in this situation is what motivates the manipulators, that is, what are their values?—since, as Courtenay says, "Nobody should play with lives the way we do unless he's motivated by the highest ideals." But the only ideal he can think of is "Sales!" [7] Indeed, again and again, the space merchants confirm the prediction that the utopians, once they have seen through human nature, will have nothing except their impulses and desires to guide them. Thus the space merchants have absolutely no scruples about projecting advertisements in a way which constitutes a safety hazard, or pushing a product, even among children, which is harmful or habit-forming. Perhaps the greatest evidence of the lack of values among the space merchants is Courtenay's reaction to statistics in *Biometrika* (the handbook of the copy-smith) about such things as changes in population and intelligence. "Almost every issue had good news for us," he remarks. "Increase of population was always good news to us. More people, more sales. Decrease of IQ was always good news to us. Less brains, more sales." [8] Altogether *The Space Merchants* demonstrates that in its evolution into popular literature the counter-Wellsian anti-utopia retained considerable vitality.

More obviously Wellsian is Bradbury's excellent *Fahrenheit 451*, an anti-utopia for which Amis has considerable praise: "The book emerges quite creditably from a comparison with *Nineteen Eighty-four* as inferior in power, but superior in conciseness and objectivity." [9] Actually what we have in *Fahrenheit 451* is the *Brave New World* kind of anti-Wellsianism brought up to date to fit a post-atomic bomb, post-World War II age. As such it is almost the archetypal anti-utopia of the new era in which we live.

While the jet bombers boom overhead and another nuclear war threatens, Americans live a mindless life in a society where everyone is encouraged to lose himself in such distractions as four-wall television, hearing-aid radios, high-speed travel, and group sports. Life is reduced to the paste-pudding norm of a mass audience, for it serves the purpose of the government to keep people from thinking:

School is shortened, discipline relaxed, philosophies, histories, languages dropped, English and spelling gradually neglected, finally almost completely ignored. Life is immediate, the job counts, pleasure lies all about after work. Why learn anything save pressing buttons, pulling switches, fixing nuts and bolts? [10]

The gadgets are, of course, marvelous and everywhere, while the greatest enemies of the status quo are books, which, when they are occasionally discovered, are burned by firemen who are, in this fireproof age, no longer needed to put out fires, but to set them (hence the title, for 451° is the temperature at which paper burns). But, as is customary in anti-utopia, there is an effort at rebellion—in this case a small group of men, living usually in the woods and forests, commit to memory as much of man's written heritage as they can. And as usual, there is a hero who in the course of the book is converted to the cause of the rebels. At the end, the threatened nuclear holocaust takes place and the rebels are about all that is left of man's heritage.

But the best of the science-fiction anti-utopias—and indeed the best of all the recent anti-utopias—is Vonnegut's brilliantly satiric *Player Piano*. At the same time it is the most Wellsian—or anti-Wellsian—because it presents, though not consciously in reference to Wells, a final critique of the Wellsian dream of a society run by an elite of functional people, i.e. managers and engineers, as well as a final critique of the Wellsian love of machines and efficiency. It is final in the sense that it projects the Wellsian vision into our coming automated civilization.

Vonnegut sets his novel in the not-too-distant future, after World War III, when America has solved the problems of production and distribution and all people, even the lowest of citizens, have complete security and abundance of physical comforts: cradle-to-the-grave medical care and guaranteed annual wage; 27-inch television sets, ultrasonic dishwashers, glass and steel houses. All this, of course, has come about because of a Second Industrial Revolution (in terminology as well as ideas Vonnegut is indebted to Norbert Wiener), a revolution which is the ultimate expression of the American gadgeteer mentality. Indeed, America has become one stupendous machine: automation has replaced human workers; managers and engineers run the economy and government with the help of *Epicac XIV*, a giant electronic brain; and people are rigidly assigned jobs and opportunities for advanced education on the basis of their marks on nationally administered, machine-scored aptitude tests. To the ruling managers and engineers, who naïvely believe that material goods alone make happiness and who fail to recognize that so many of their fellow men are leading "lives of quiet desperation," "Civilization has reached the dizziest of heights"; but to the great mass of people, life has never been duller and more meaningless—the people, that is, who, because their test scores do not qualify them for any important position in society, are sent, to keep them busy, into either the Army for twenty-five years or into the Reclamation and Reconstruction Corps, an organization devoted to jobs not profitably performed by machines, such as filling in the holes in the streets. Perhaps the most depressing sections of the book are those which describe the monotonous life of the mass of people, who are packed away in standardized houses and whose chief source of entertainment is television. The life of the managers and engineers is also shallow, though they generally lack the self-perception necessary to realize this and they also have the satisfaction of their work, which at least challenges them and gives some meaning to existence. In time, however, the tension between the elite and the masses leads to rebellion, a rebellion organized by a secret society and using one of the leading engineers as a figurehead. Although the rebellion is successful for a while and results in the riotous destruction of most of the machines in a few cities, it ultimately fails, but not before the rebels have started tinkering with the machines and putting them together again—an event which underscores Vonnegut's pessimism about the American character.

The novel contains many of the familiar features of the counter-Wellsian anti-utopia. As usual, society is a pyramid topped by an elite, with the great mass of people faceless and nameless—the line of descent runs direct from the blue-clad workers of Wells's Labour Company through Huxley's Gammas, Deltas, and Epsilons to Orwell's Proles. As usual the elite rules with the help of a strong police force, who employ the latest, most efficient means of surveillance. As usual, there is a rebellion, which, again as usual, fails. There is even the traditional escape to nature, when the hero, dreaming of a more primitive life, buys an old, unmechanized farm on which he hopes to live. And as usual it pictures a machine civilization, one in which machines are replacing men. The only difference between Vonnegut's nightmare and its ancestors is that Vonnegut's seems closer to coming reality as we may come to know it. It is here that *Player Piano* makes it most profound comment.

Vonnegut saw two ways in which machines are replacing men. One is that the production of goods by automated machines has not only taken away from human beings the pleasure of working with their hands, but also, even more important, has led to the situation in which for many men there is nothing that they can contribute, nothing useful that they can do. The other way in which machines have replaced human beings is in the making of decisions, a process which began when the thinking machines became smarter than men. *Epicac XIV*, the electronic brain which really governs, is always completely free of emotion and so immensely intelligent that it can solve problems which it would take the most brilliant core of American genius, with boundless resources and the most highly inspired leadership, thousands of years. It is, therefore, not surprising that *Epicac XIV* is always deferred to, and naturally enough, since the machine is never bothered by reason-clouding emotion, it is not surprising that its decisions often result in the non-human use of human beings, in the quantification of human problems.

It is not, however, science itself which is the villain in *Player Piano* but the development and application of technology, which has proceeded lawlessly without consideration of its effect on human life and human values. The irony of the whole thing is that man, because of automated production and thinking machines, has finally achieved the long-awaited utopia, has entered the Eden of eternal peace, but "everything he had looked forward to enjoying there, pride, dignity, self-respect, work worth doing, has been condemned as unfit for human consumption." [11] And so in *Player Piano* we have the best of the recent anti-utopias and at the same time the most profoundly anti-Wellsian.

EPILOGUE

F *acial Justice* and *Player Piano*, easily the most important anti-utopias written since *Nineteen Eighty-four*, might well be the last flowering of the anti-utopian tradition before its disintegration. And yet they are very Wellsian, in spite of the lapse of so many years since the period of Wells's greatest influence. That *Player Piano* and *Facial Justice*, as well as the other postwar anti-utopias, are still Wellsian appears less surprising when it is realized that Wells's impact also extends to a number of works, likewise recent, which are not strictly anti-utopias but are only science fiction, anti-utopian in spirit. One of the most important of these is William Golding's *The Inheritors* (1955), a book whose relationship to Wells has at last received the attention it deserves in Bernard Oldsey and Stanley Weintraub's excellent *The Art of William Golding.*[1] I should note here, before going on to *The Inheritors*, that Golding, like C. S. Lewis, is a long-time reader of science fiction, including the magazines, though he now claims to regard his lifelong addiction as largely a waste.[2] Nevertheless, this interest led him to write, besides *The Inheritors*, a science-fiction novella, "Envoy Extraordinary," which tells how a Roman emperor rejects gunpowder, the steam engine, and printing, and sends their inventor to China.[3]

The Inheritors is representative of one of the two kinds of science fiction which Amis added as codicils to his definition of the genre because they appeal to the same set of interests or are written and read by the same writers and readers—in this case, stories about prehistoric man. Amis has suggested that stories in this category all go back to Wells's "A Story of the Stone Age" (1897), and this is probably true of *The Inheritors*, although, of course, the more immediate ancestors of Golding's novel are parts of Wells's *Outline of History* (first published in 1920), and his other story about prehistoric man, "The Grisly Folk" (first published in 1921 though perhaps written not long after Wells finished the *Outline*). "A Story of the Stone Age" tells of the courage and ingenuity of Ugh-lomi and his woman, Eudena, who succeed in their fight to stay alive, and finally defeat the persecutions of the chief of the tribe. Ultimately Ugh-lomi becomes chief himself. The story vividly recreates the psychology of paleolithic man and sees in him and the qualities of his mind the beginnings of civilization and science.

In the *Outline of History* and in "The Grisly Folk," Wells expanded the theme of "A Story of the Stone Age" to describe the encounter of these paleolithic "True Men" (*homo sapiens*) with Neanderthal men. As the last ice age abates, the True Men move up from the great valley which is now the Mediterranean and discover the Neanderthalers living in the shadows of the retreating glaciers. The primitive Neanderthal men are, of course, annihilated by the more intelligent and more highly organized True Men in the conflict which inevitably ensues. Essentially this is also the story of *The Inheritors*, but Golding's sympathies were antithetic to Wells's and he inverted the story to attack the Wellsian vision.

The essential difference between Wells's and Golding's views of the two species and the encounter between them was succinctly described by Peter Green when he contrasted "The Grisly Folk" with *The Inheritors*:

In this tale all Wells's sympathies, as we might expect, are with *homo sapiens*, humanity, achievement, discovery, progress. The Neanderthalers are huge, half-witted, cruel monsters: one of them steals a human child, and Wells exults in their hunting down and ultimate destruction.[4]

Golding himself also contrasted his conception with the rationalist basis of Wells's view of Neanderthal man, particularly as it manifests itself in *The Outline of History*:

Wells's *Outline* played a great part in my life because my father was a rationalist, and the *Outline* was something he took neat. It is the rationalist gospel *in excelsis*. . . . By and by it seemed to me not to be large enough . . . too neat and too slick. And when I re-read it as an adult I came across his picture of Neanderthal man, our immediate predecessors, as being those gross brutal creatures who were possibly the basis of the mythological bad man [i.e. ogre]. . . . I thought to myself that this is just absurd. . . .[5]

Golding used as an ironic epigraph for *The Inheritors* a quotation from *The Outline of History* in which it is suggested that the dim racial memory of the repulsive, beetle-browed Neanderthaler is the germ of the ogre in folklore.

And so *The Inheritors* tells how eight Neanderthalers— six adults, a small girl, and an infant who come up from caves by the sea to spend the spring and summer by a great waterfall—are killed off, except for one adult and the kidnapped infant, by a party of ruthless and aggressive *homo sapiens*. Except for the last chapter, the story is narrated from the point of view of the simple and innocent Neanderthalers, who love each other and think only in "pictures," never rising to concepts. They are hopelessly outclassed by the *homo sapiens*, with their superior intelligence and the beginnings of civilization, including bows and arrows and dugout canoes. The chief theme of *The Inheritors* is, of course, the familiar one of the corruption of human nature, the fall of man. In this respect there is some truth—along with perhaps some bias—in Martin Green's statement:

. . . Golding is a belated recruit to the ranks of those writers who have rediscovered for this century man's essential savagery; who have triumphantly rejected science and hygiene, liberalism and progress; who have, in any account of contemporary conditions, alternated between effects of commonplaceness and effects of nightmare· He is so belated as to inherit these themes in their decrepitude.[6]

Still, *The Inheritors* is a vigorous counterthrust to Wells, and as such it is related to the major anti-utopias of the twentieth century. And like them it borrows from Wells, not only the basic plot, as we have seen, but also various details. There is, for example, as Peter Green noted, the kidnapping of the child, which Golding took from "The Grisly Folk," but which he inverted by having *homo sapiens* take the Neanderthal children. Then, the ledge on which the Neanderthalers live in *The Inheritors* comes right out of "A Story of the Stone Age" and "The Grisly Folk." [7] There are more than enough of these borrowings to establish that, although Golding dislikes Wells's philosophy, he has been captured by the Wellsian imagination.

Before leaving Golding one should note that his much more famous first novel, *The Lord of the Flies*, which makes much the same point as *The Inheritors,* is at least akin to science fiction. It is a kind of *Robinsonade,* and particularly an inversion of R. M. Ballantyne's children's classic, *The Coral Island.* But in its use of the desert island myth—what Gerber called the English island myth—to delineate the savagery in human nature, *The Lord of the Flies* echoes, though it never directly imitates, that most pessimistic of Wells's scientific romances, *The Island of Dr. Moreau.* At the same time its portrayal of the savagery to which the children revert is very much like the savagery of the *homo sapiens* in *The Inheritors*—in other words, it is a variety of the story of our prehistoric ancestors. Finally, because the adventures of the refugee children on the desert island takes place against the background of a great atomic war, *The Lord of the Flies* is also a post-catastrophe novel.

II

Indeed, the story of the catastrophic end of civilization is a form of Wellsian science fiction which, in these nuclear years, may be replacing the anti-utopia proper as a vehicle of diagnosis and warning. It is related, of course, to the anti-utopia, for in many of the major anti-utopias the great World State, following Wells's prediction, comes into existence after a disastrous world war and the collapse of civilization. This disaster and collapse can also be the chief story itself, as in Albert Guerard's *Night Journey* (1950), which tells of an endless, purposeless, undeclared war waged by deteriorating armies that take and retake cities and towns, reducing Europe to rubble and its peoples to starvation. One of the most important of such stories, Huxley's *Ape and Essence,* we have already discussed. But there are others which need to be touched upon as we trace the continuing impact of the Wellsian imagination.

The post-catastrophe story, which usually tells also of mankind's return to savagery, is not solely Wellsian in its origins. There is no question that it could in part be traced back to such works as the anonymous *Omegarus and Syderia; or The Last Man: A Romance of Futurity* (1806), Mary Shelley's *The Last Man* (1825), or the more recent and better known—at least in England—*After London* (1885) by Richard Jefferies. Sometimes the post-catastrophe story can be included in the category of invasion stories popular after Chesney's "Battle of Dorking." But surely it is the pictures of world collapse given by Wells in such works as *The War of the Worlds, The War in the Air*, or *The World Set Free* that have most influenced the development of this kind of story in the twentieth century. In some stories civilization is brought to an end by other causes, such as a great plague, as is the case in Jack London's "The Scarlet Plague" and George R. Stewart's *Earth Abides*. And in other stories, such as Stephen Vincent Benét's "By the Waters of Babylon" and Jefferies's *After London*, we are shown mankind reverted to barbarism without any clear explanation of why this has happened.

But the stories with which we are concerned here are the recent apocalyptic ones, like *Ape and Essence*, whose chief concern is to show modern war, usually nuclear, bringing or threatening the end of civilization. These are the ones which are more directly the heirs to the Wellsian imagination and which seem to have the vitality which the anti-utopia has lost. Since Hiroshima, stories of this kind have appeared in great numbers (though one of the best of them, Walter Van Tilburg Clark's "The Portable Phonograph," was published almost on the eve of Pearl Harbor). They represent an astonishing range in literary accomplishment—everything from Nevil Shute's *On the Beach* and Eugene Burdick's *Fail Safe* to Clark's "The Portable Phonograph" and Graham

Greene's "A Discovery in the Woods." And in the case of the satiric *Dr. Strangelove*, the form has been brilliantly adapted to another medium, the film.

The chief warning of most recent apocalyptic stories is that man has "outrun his intelligence," that man is not good enough to survive in the world created by his science and technology. Out of the great multitude of such stories, four deserve at least brief comment here. They fall neatly into two categories: two are short stories by established and distinguished writers—"The Portable Phonograph" (1941) by Clark and "A Discovery in the Woods" (1963) by Graham Greene—and two are novels by "professional" science-fiction writers—*Re-Birth* (1953) by John Wyndham and *A Canticle for Leibowitz* (1959) by Walter M. Miller, Jr. "A Discovery in the Woods" and "The Portable Phonograph" represent a similar evolution from the Wellsian post-catastrophe novel in that both attempt to portray the feelings of those who come after the disaster and the quality of their life, and so comment more subtly on the significance of the disaster. But they are, of course, two very different stories.

In "The Portable Phonograph" four cultured men, who are barely able to survive in caves on a desolate, frozen plain after a cataclysmic war, attempt to hang on to the memory of the life of the mind and spirit which they have irretrievably lost. One of the men, Dr. Jenkins, reads to the others from the books he has managed to save—Shakespeare, the Bible, *Moby-Dick*, *The Divine Comedy*—and plays for them records on a portable phonograph. The pathos of their longing for what has been lost is movingly captured, as is the desolation that provides the background:

Out of the sunset, through the dead, matted grass and isolated weed stalks of the prairie, crept the narrow and deeply rutted remains of a road. In the road, in places, there were crusts of shallow, brittle ice.

There were little islands of an old oiled pavement in the road too, but most of it was mud, now frozen rigid. The frozen mud still bore the toothed impress of great tanks, and a wanderer on the neighboring undulations might have stumbled, in this light, into large, partially filled-in and weed-grown cavities, their banks channeled and beginning to spread into badlands. These pits were such as might have been made by falling meteors, but they were not. They were the scars of gigantic bombs, their rawness already made a little natural by rain, seed and time. Along the road there were rakish remnants of fence. There was also, just visible, one portion of tangled and multiple barbed wire still erect, behind which was a shelving ditch with small caves, now very quiet and empty, at intervals in its back wall. Otherwise there was no structure or remnant of a structure visible over the dome of the darkling earth, but only, in sheltered hollows, the darker shadows of young trees trying again.[8]

"A Discovery in the Woods" takes us an indefinite number of years (it could be a thousand) into a time after the great catastrophe, to meet our descendants—little people about four feet tall, incapable of even the simplest intellectual activity, who live in a fishing village (called Bottom) near the sea about twenty miles from another such village, together the only known settlements of man. Their world is a vast, unexplored wilderness, and the story deals with the escapade of five blackberry hunting children who wander beyond the limits set by custom and discover what we realize is the wreck of a great ocean liner. Finally they come upon a skeleton, and the little girl cries because men are no longer giants:

She leant forward towards the gaping mouth. "He's beautiful," she said, "he's so beautiful. And he's a giant. Why aren't there giants now?" She began to keen over him like a little old woman at a funeral. "He's six feet tall," she cried, exaggerating a little, "and he has beautiful straight legs. No one has straight legs in Bottom. Why aren't there giants now? Look at his lovely mouth with all the teeth. Who has teeth like that in Bottom?" [9]

The two post-catastrophe novels—Wyndham's *Re-Birth* and Miller's *A Canticle for Leibowitz*—also represent an evolution from the Wellsian story of war and world collapse, but they are much closer to Wells than are "The Portable Phonograph" or "A Discovery in the Woods," chiefly because they are "future histories," works of greater scope in which idea is generally more important than characterization. Wyndham and Miller are much less concerned with portraying the quality and texture of life than they are in making comment on it and in warning us where we are headed.

Re-Birth takes us into the future a thousand years after Tribulation, the atomic disaster of the twentieth century, to a district of now temperate Labrador, where the inhabitants, who seem to be at the level of civilization of perhaps seventeenth-century America, are frantically carrying out God's command to preserve the purity of living things. Offenses, mutations among animals and plants, are destroyed, while Blasphemies, deviations among people, are driven into the Fringes, a bordering area with a higher deviation rate, where the refugees become savages, making periodic raids on nearby settlements. The process of preserving original forms is blindly and ruthlessly carried out without regard either for principles of humanity or for common sense, as in the case of harmless mutations, where even otherwise normal children are forced to flee when they are discovered to be endowed with six toes. In spite of the stupidity and inhumanity of so many of their actions, the people of Labrador believe that they are in the process of climbing back into Grace, of attaining the peaks from which mankind had fallen because of Tribulation; and the reward of God's forgiveness will be restoration of the Golden Age of the Old People. In *Re-Birth* Wyndham makes it abundantly clear through the activities of the people of Labrador that, once they achieved the level of civilization of the Old People, they would likewise destroy themselves.

The ending of *Re-Birth* underlines its central idea: that man as he now exists is an inadequate species which must be superseded if the world is to survive. The young protagonists of the novel are forced to flee to the Fringes when they are discovered to be mutations: they possess the ability to communicate without words. Moments before capture, they are rescued by a party of similarly telepathic people, who have tuned in on the signals of the young mutants in Labrador and have flown across the world's vast radioactive Badlands from their island community far to the south (called Zealand). Because their new dimension of mind enables them to think collectively, the Zealanders have constructed an advanced, utopian civilization. Their spokesman explains why the Old People, whose descendants live in primitive backwaters like Labrador, must give way to this next stage in evolution:

When their conditions were primitive they could get along all right, as the animals can; but the more complex they made their world, the less capable they were of dealing with it. They had no means of concensus. They learnt to cooperate constructively in small units; but only destructively in large units. They aspired greedily, and then refused to face the responsibilities. . . . There was, you see, no real communication, no understanding between them. They could, at their best, be near-sublime animals, but not more.[10]

Though the novel holds out a utopian ideal in the achievements of the Zealanders, it offers no hope that man as he is now constituted can ever achieve that ideal. We, said Wyndham, are the Old People, and eventually we will bring down Tribulation upon ourselves.

In bare synopsis, *A Canticle For Leibowitz* seems roughly similar to *Re-Birth*. After the great Flame Deluge, the

nuclear holocaust of the 1960's, mankind reverts to ignorance and savagery. It is another Dark Age, and only the
Catholic Church, and particularly the monks of the Al-
bertian Order of Leibowitz, manage to keep a tiny flame of
knowledge burning and preserve the few books and documents that were not destroyed in the great disaster or in the
Simplification, the bookburning and massacre of scientists
and educated people which followed as a natural reaction.
But finally, after many centuries, a second Renaissance
occurs, and thereafter mankind moves speedily to the level
of technology and material accomplishment of the previous
civilization. But again terrible weapons of destruction, mis-
siles and nuclear bombs, are developed. And again the greed
and ambition of men lead to the use of these weapons and to
the destruction of the world. But this time, just before the
end, a starship leaves with nuns, children, priests, and three
bishops to take the soul and substance of man to another
world—"a new Exodus from Egypt under the auspices of a
God who must surely be very weary of the race of Man."
Such a synopsis does not, of course, capture the unique qualities of the book—its irony and wit, its compassionate
humor. It is an extremely persuasive presentation of the idea
that now, as never before, fallen man must live by the Judaic-
Christian ethic.

III

At a time when the anti-utopia has lost its initial vitality and
come to be replaced by its mutation, the apocalyptic novel,
it is possible to find the first signs of a coming revival of that
other Wellsian form, the utopia. One such indication is
George Kateb's recent, brilliant book, *Utopia and its
Enemies* (1963)—a closely reasoned defense of the idea of
utopia against all its major critics, from Dostoevsky to

Huxley. Kateb defended what he describes in the following paragraph as "modern utopianism":

> Imagine a society in which all conflicts of conscience and conflicts of interest were abolished, a society in which all the obstacles to a decent life for all men had been removed, all the hindrances hindered, a society in which the resourcefulness of modern technology was put in the unfettered service of lessening labor and increasing and enriching leisure, a society in which the advances in biological and psychological science were used to correct the work of nature and improve the species, a society in which peace, abundance, and virtue permanently and universally obtained. Such a society answers to the traditional ends of utopianism, at the same time that it bodies them forth in ways undreamt of by the tradition. Such a society not only presupposes a technology that could, for the first time, make utopianism something more than a hopeless and recurrent nostalgia, but also amplifies and elevates those things which utopianism, in its vision of perfection, has always stood for. Such a society is what we shall mean by modern utopianism.[11]

Another indication of utopia's revival, and one which followed closely upon Kateb's book and which may well have been triggered by it, is the publication in Spring 1965 of an issue of *Daedalus* devoted to "utopia." [12] Its articles were written by such distinguished scholars as Lewis Mumford, Northrop Frye, Crane Brinton, and Judith Shklar, and, although the various writers are not always sympathetic to the idea of utopia, the issue taken over-all indeed suggests a new and growing interest in the subject. Most of the writers are social scientists who are concerned with utopia as a way of looking at man in society (as Wells proposed in "The So-Called Science of Sociology").

Finally, as an indication of a revival, three important utopias, the first to be written since Wells's *A Modern Utopia*, have appeared in recent years—B. F. Skinner's *Walden Two* in 1948, one year before Orwell's nightmare; the Russian Ivan Yefremov's *Andromeda* in 1957; and Aldous Huxley's *Island* in 1962. *Walden Two* is the famous—or infamous, depending on one's point of view—paradise of the behavioral psychologist, where competitiveness and aggressiveness are eliminated and men are conditioned to be good. Some indication of its importance are the number of criticisms it has elicited, the most important being the extended attack by Joseph Wood Krutch in *The Measure of Man*. *Andromeda* is a powerful, though occasionally crude, answer to anti-utopianism by the country which silenced Zamyatin. And *Island*, as we have seen, is the utopian recantation of the century's most cynical—and perhaps most brilliant—anti-utopian: Huxley's last major statement on the subject before his death. Although all three books represent new directions in utopian writing, the influence of the Wellsian imagination still persists. In this respect they are only a short step from the anti-utopias we have studied.

Although Skinner is heavily indebted to Bellamy's *Looking Backward*, particularly for the idea of different labor credits to be assigned to different kinds of work, he very evidently shares with Wells a great number of values and ideas and takes from Wells's utopias and scientific romances various details. Whether Skinner borrowed consciously from Wells would be difficult to show, though he certainly knows Wells's work and referred to it once at least in *Walden Two*. At any rate, Skinner is as much a rationalist as Wells and believes as wholeheartedly in the application of the scientific method. And like Wells he values change and the forward movement of mankind:

"Could you really be happy in a static world, no matter how satisfying it might be in other respects?" Frazier went on. "By no means! Nor would you wish to engineer general happiness for everyone under static conditions. We must never be free of that feverish urge to push forward which is the saving grace of mankind." [13]

And like Wells he dreams of Man taking charge of Man and ultimately creating Men Like Gods:

"My hunch is—and when I feel this about a hunch, it's never wrong—that we shall eventually find out, not only what makes a child mathematical, but how to make better mathematicians! If we can't solve a problem, we can create men who can! And better artists! And better craftsmen!" [14]

It is not surprising, then, that many of the details of life in *Walden Two* are Wellsian. Thus the bonds of the family are weakened and children are raised in "Skinner boxes" and nurseries, arrangements more than reminiscent of Wells's crèches. And, as with Wells, the private home has disappeared and people live in personal rooms, like those in hotels, eat in communal dining rooms, and relax in the common rooms, theater, and library. Very Wellsian also is the way in which the community is managed: there is no democracy, but instead an elite of planners, managers, and scientists who co-ordinate, investigate, and administer. In many ways *Walden Two* is a Wellsian utopia.

But *Walden Two* develops an idea which is only vaguely drawn in Wells's *Men Like Gods*, although its essence is contained in the slogan of that book, "Our education is our government." Using the theory of positive reinforcement and the supporting techniques of behavioral engineering, the functional elite of *Walden Two* rule for the greatest happiness of all by making people want to do what they are supposed to do. *Walden Two* is a psychological utopia, in a way that is not true of Wells's utopias, even *Men Like Gods*. For Skinner, as it was not true for Wells, the chief problems in creating and maintaining a utopia are psychological:

No one can seriously doubt that a well-managed community will get along successfully as an economic unit. A child could prove it. The real problems are psychological. [15]

Although it has some features of a psychological utopia, Yefremov's *Andromeda* is a different sort of work from *Walden Two*. More of a romance, its descriptions of utopia are set in the framework of adventures in the future: heroic journeys into deep space and landings on strange worlds; archaelogical excavations to unearth the artifacts of the twentieth century; visits to the bottom of the sea, subterranean mines, and the great protein forests of the tropics; television transmission to planets circling distant suns.

Yet with all these features, the book has a didactic purpose: to affirm certain values and ideals of Soviet society, which are surprisingly Wellsian. (The Soviet literary historian, J. Kagarlitski, has noted that Wells, who has always been read in Russia, is now enjoying something of a boom.[16]) Today Russia apparently finds the Wellsian vision extremely congenial, and, since the Communist party reversed its stand on fantasy, the government has been encouraging books like *Andromeda*.[17]

In its utopian passages, *Andromeda* seems a re-write of *A Modern Utopia* and *Men Like Gods*. The resemblances are extraordinary, and, except for its dialectical view of history, it is pure Wells. Yefremov portrays a great World State, employing science and technology in the service of man. For his utopians, there is no way but knowledge out of the cages of life: "The Sun is the incarnation of the bright forces of the intellect driving away the darkness and monsters of night." [18] The dissolving of the worst of egotisms has been accomplished, and Yefremov's utopians are educated and conditioned from childhood to master their selfhood and substitute a social conscience. They believe that man—"that beautiful and intelligent being"—is the measure. Even their attitude towards nature is Huxleyan in the manner of Wells: savage and ruthless, it must be checked and controlled. The goal of their World State is to end human drudgery and mindless labor, pain and unnecessary misery, war and destructive forms of competition so that the human spirit may be freed for new adventure and new creativity. They have no *samurai,* of course, because this is a utopia at the later stage of *Men Like Gods.* Besides these basic features, many smaller details derive from Wells (taken largely from *A Modern Utopia*) such as a 200-kilometer-per-hour train, an Island of Oblivion, and clean, functional buildings.

Internal evidence suggests that, as an answer to anti-utopianism, *Andromeda* is consciously so. One of Yefremov's characters, for example, speaks of the nightmare worlds—ours had been one earlier—"where the highest achievements of science were used to intimidate, for torture and punishment, for thought-reading and turning the masses into obedient semi-idiots ever ready to fulfill the most monstrous orders." [19] Yefremov is showing us the alternative which could be wrought by the intelligent use of science and the reorganization of the world along socialist lines.

With *Island* we return to a much more polished work. Like *Walden Two,* it is more of a psychological utopia, but in a manner of greater significance for the future of the genre, at least in the West. As Kateb himself pointed out in "Utopia and the Good Life" (in the Spring 1965 issue of *Daedalus*), *Island* is a "very imaginative effort" to project a way of life similar in many respects to the one Herbert Marcuse conceived in *Eros and Civilization.*[20] That is to say, *Island* is a utopia in which the libido is freed and aggressiveness is ended because men have been emancipated from economic and sexual repression. One gathers from certain of the essays in *Daedalus,* particularly Kateb's "Utopia and the Good Life" and Frank E. Manuel's "Toward a Psychological History of Utopias," that dreams, not of reason, but of "psychic self-actualization" might well be the form which a revival of utopia will take in an abundant, affluent society where men have been totally freed from labor by the means of automated production. And *Island,* with its consciousness-expanding *moksha-medicine,* its hypnotism for Destiny Control, and its yoga of love may well have set the pattern for a series of subsequent utopias of this sort. If *Island* should so set the pattern for the future, then behind this new phenomenon, though admittedly at a distance, will also stand Wells, for *Island* is directly descended, through *Brave New World*, from *Men Like Gods* and is as much a scientific romance as any of the great anti-utopias we have studied. Thus the swing of the pendulum from anti-utopia to utopia may prove to be as Wellsian in the last analysis as the preceding swing from utopia to anti-utopia.

CHAPTER I

1. Dickinson is quoted in Forster, *Goldsworthy Lowes Dickinson* (London, 1934), p. 217; Orwell, *Road to Wigan Pier* (London, 1937), p. 225; and Lewis, *The Writer and the Absolute* (London, 1952), p. 154.
2. "Technique as Discovery," in William Van O'Connor (ed.), *Forms of Modern Fiction*, (Minneapolis, 1948), p. 15.
3. "Wells, Hitler and the World State" in *Dickens, Dali and Others* (New York, 1946), p. 121.
4. "Passing of a Utopian," August 14, 1946, p. 24.
5. *Eight Modern Writers* (Oxford, 1963), pp. 11–12.
6. *Science and the Shabby Curate of Poetry* (New York, 1965), p. 4.
7. New York, 1960, p. 18.
8. *Jules Verne* (London, 1940).

9. Leon Edel and Gordon Ray (eds.), *Henry James and H. G. Wells* (Urbana, 1958), p. 80.
10. G. Jean-Aubry (ed.), *Joseph Conrad: Life and Letters* (New York, 1927), I, 259.
11. *Review of Reviews*, XI (1895), 263; *Spectator*, January 29, 1898, p. 168.
12. *The World of H.G. Wells* (New York, 1915).
13. *Nature*, LXV, 326.
14. Ibid. 331.

CHAPTER II

1. See, for example, W. T. Stead, "The Latest Apocalypse of the End of the World," *Review of Reviews*, XVII (1898), 389–96. Many other such reviews are listed in Ingvald Raknem, *H. G. Wells and His Critics* (Oslo, 1962).
2. *H. G. Wells: A Sketch for a Portrait* (New York, 1930), p. 106.
3. *H. G. Wells* (Denver, 1950), p. 32.
4. VII (February 1957), 52–9.
5. Manchester, England, 1961.
6. See C. F. G. Masterman, *The Condition of England* (London, 1909); and Élie Halévy, *A History of the English People in the Nineteenth Century*, V and VI (New York, 1961).
7. See Hillegas, "Cosmic Pessimism in H. G. Wells's Scientific Romances," *Papers of the Michigan Academy*, XLVI (1960), 655–63.
8. Quoted by Geoffrey West in *H. G. Wells*, p. 49.
9. "Scepticism of the Instrument," in *A Modern Utopia* (London, 1905), p. 376.
10. *H. G. Wells and the World State* (New Haven, 1961), p. 17.
11. Major statements of Huxley's cosmic pessimism can be found in his "The Struggle for Existence in Human Society," *Nineteenth Century*, XXIII (February 1888), 161–80; "Agnosticism," *Saturday Review*, XXV (February 1889), 168–94; "Government: Anarchy or Regimentation," *Nineteenth Century*, XXVII (May 1890), 843–66; and "Evolution and Ethics," *Evolution and Ethics and Other Essays* (London, 1894).
12. *Huxley, Prophet of Science* (London, 1932), p. 282.
13. "Struggle for Existence in Human Society," p. 163.
14. *Certain Personal Matters* (London, 1897), p. 173.

15. Ibid. pp. 178–9.
16. See Hillegas, "The First Invasions from Mars," *Michigan Alumnus Quarterly Review*, LXVI (February 1960), 107–12.
17. London, 1966.
18. *The Scientific Romances of H. G. Wells*, Introduction to the Gollancz edition (London, 1933), p. viii.
19. For a discussion of time travel and its relationship to the cosmic voyage, see Hillegas, "The Cosmic Voyage and the Doctrine of Inhabited Worlds in Nineteenth-Century English Literature" (unpub. diss., Columbia University, 1957).
20. "Evolution and Ethics," p. 86.
21. New York, 1958, pp. 136–7.
22. *H. G. Wells*, p. 28.
23. *From Utopia to Nightmare* (New York and Evanston, 1962), pp. 74–5.
24. *H. G. Wells*, p. 31.
25. *Early H. G. Wells*, pp. 104–5.
26. Ibid. p. 108.
27. Quoted by Geoffrey West, p. 104.

CHAPTER III

1. *From the Abyss* (London, 1902).
2. New York, 1934, pp. 550–51.
3. *Utopian Fantasy* (London, 1955), p. 62.
4. This passage is cited by Gerber.
5. A perceptive analysis of Wells's technique in *The First Men in the Moon* can be found in Norman Nicholson's *H. G. Wells*, pp. 22–5.
6. See Marjorie Nicolson, *Voyages to the Moon* (New York, 1948), pp. 249–50; and Coleman O. Parsons, "Lunar Craters in Science and Fiction," *Notes and Queries*, CLXIV (1933), 346–8.

CHAPTER IV

1. "The Late Mr. Wells," *Prejudices: First Series* (New York, 1919), p. 28.
2. *An Englishman Looks at the World* (London, 1914), p. 199.
3. Ibid. p. 205.

4. *The World Set Free* (London, 1914), p. 137.
5. *Experiment in Autobiography*, p. 564.
6. *H. G. Wells*, p. 164.
7. Henry James praises A *Modern Utopia* in his famous letter to Wells of November 19, 1905 (*Henry James and H. G. Wells*, pp. 102–7); Conrad in a letter to Wells of April 25, 1905 (*Joseph Conrad: Life and Letters*, II, 15–16); William James in a letter to Wells of June 6, 1905 (Henry James [ed.], *The Letters of William James* [Boston, 1920], II, 231).
8. See Marie Louise Berneri, *Journey Through Utopia* (London, 1950); Richard Gerber, *Utopian Fantasy* (London, 1955); J. O. Hertzler, *The History of Utopian Thought* (New York, 1923); Frank Manuel, (ed.), *Utopias and Utopian Thought* (Boston, 1966); A. L. Morton, *The English Utopia* (London, 1952); Lewis Mumford, *The Story of Utopias* (New York, 1962); Glenn Negley and J. Max Patrick, *The Quest for Utopia* (Garden City, N.Y., 1962); Frances Theresa Russell, *Touring Utopia* (New York, 1932); Chad Walsh, *From Utopia to Nightmare* (New York and Evanston, 1962).
9. *H. G. Wells*, p. 162.
10. *The Story of Utopias* (New York, 1962), p. 184 and p. 171.
11. *New Atlantis* (London, 1730), p. 253.

CHAPTER V

1. Published in the *Oxford and Cambridge Review* in 1909 (Michaelmas Term).
2. The Socialist *Tribune*, January 4, 1946.
3. "Utopias in Negative," *Sewanee Review*, LXIV (1956), 85.
4. *The End of Our Time* (London, 1933), p. 188.
5. London, 1928, p. 290.
6. *H. G. Wells and the World State*, p. 238.
7. *Spectator*, December 11, 1936, p. 1033.
8. *The Collected Tales of E. M. Forster* (New York, 1947), p. vii; Trilling, *E. M. Forster* (Norfolk, Conn., 1943), p. 47; and *Goldsworthy Lowes Dickinson*, p. 217.
9. *E. M. Forster: The Perils of Humanism* (Princeton, 1962), p. 5.
10. *Two Cheers for Democracy* (London, 1951), p. 68.
11. *Perils of Humanism*, p. 38.
12. Ibid. p. 36.

13. In his essay on *Erewhon*—"A Book that Influenced Me"—
    Forster notes that "what he [Butler] had to say was congenial,
    and I lapped it up." As to technique, Forster says *Erewhon* also
    influenced him: "I like that idea of fantasy, of muddling up the
    actual and the impossible until the reader isn't sure which is
    which." Finally, he praises *Erewhon* over *Gulliver*: "Swift's in-
    dignation in *Gulliver* is too savage for me. I prefer Butler's in
    Erewhon" (*Two Cheers*, pp. 227–8).
14. *The English Utopia* (London, 1932), p. 198.
15. *The Cave and the Mountain: A Study of E. M. Forster* (Stan-
    ford, 1966), p. 152.
16. For a fascinating psychoanalytical discussion of the robot, see
    Robert Plank, "The Golem and the Robot," *Literature and
    Psychology*, XV (1965), 12–28.
17. "The Meaning of R.U.R.," *Saturday Review*, CXXXVI (July 21,
    1923), 79.
18. B. R. Bradbrook, "Letters to England from Karel Čapek,"
    Slavonic and East European Review, XXXIX (December 1960),
    64–5.
19. New York, 1962, p. 85.
20. *Times Literary Supplement* (July 5, 1923), p. 456.
21. When *Herbert Wells* first appeared in 1922 it was issued by
    the publishing house *Epokha* [Epoch] in Petersburg; slightly
    revised, it appeared again as the introduction to Wells's col-
    lected works published by the house Mysl' [Thought] in Lenin-
    grad in 1924. It is this second, revised version which is re-
    published in *Litsa* [Faces], a collection of Zamyatin's critical es-
    says. With one exception, all citations in this book are to
    Herbert Wells as published in *Litsa*.
22. A footnote in the first version of *Herbert Wells* indicates that
    Zamyatin classified *A Modern Utopia* as a "social-political, scien-
    tific and philosophical book," that is, not as fiction but as a
    work like *Anticipations* (p. 25).
23. *Modern Russian Literature* (New York, 1953), p. 291.
24. For a reading of *We* as largely a parody of *A Modern Utopia*, see
    Christopher Collins, "Zamyatin, Wells and the Utopian Literary
    Tradition," *Slavonic and East European Review*, XLIV (July
    1966), 351–60.
25. Ralph E. Matlaw (trans. and ed.), *Notes from Underground
    and the Grand Inquisitor*, (New York, 1960), p. 22.

1. George Plimpton (ed.), *Writers at Work: The Paris Review Interviews*, Second Series (New York, 1963), p. 198.
2. One could surmise that *Brave New World* is Wellsian at second remove through Zamyatin's *We*. Huxley claimed never to have read *We*, but, as Orwell pointed out in his article about *We* in the *Tribune*, the parallels between *Brave New World* are extraordinarily numerous and striking. Both describe much the same state (ruled by the same World Controller and Well-Doer), in which troublesome human freedom is taken away so that men will be happy. I consider it likely that the erudite Huxley somewhere at least heard of *We* and then forgot he had when he wrote *Brave New World*. It would not be the first or last time such a lapse occurred. The central idea of his famous essay, "Wordsworth in the Tropics," can be traced to Charles Macomb Flandrau's *Viva Mexico!*: "The poet who first apostrophized 'Mother Nature' never put on a pair of poison-proof gloves and endeavored to hack a path through jungle with a machete." More recently, the opening, as well as the setting itself, of *Island* is clearly indebted to Bernard Wolfe's anti-utopia, *Limbo*. Certainly *Brave New World* seems very indebted to *We* for Wellsian details. (Borrowings in other works by Huxley are pointed out in R. C. Bald, "Aldous Huxley as a Borrower," *College English*, XI [January 1950], 183–7.)
3. *Aldous Huxley: A Literary Study* (New York, 1956), pp. 212–16.
4. *Vanity Fair*, XXIX (January 1928), p. 105.
5. Ibid. p. 69.
6. "Spinoza's Worm," *Do What You Will* (London, 1931), p. 86.
7. Ibid. p. 88.
8. *The Road to Wigan Pier* (London, 1937), p. 225.
9. *Virginia Quarterly Review*, VII (January 1931), 49.
10. Ibid.
11. Ibid. p. 52.
12. Vol. LXXIV, p. 690.
13. Wells, with the exaggeration characteristic of his arguments with Shaw, said that, if he were standing on a pier in a storm with only one life preserver and Pavlov and Shaw were flounder-

ing in the water, he would throw the preserver to Pavlov. For an account of the controversy, see Hesketh Pearson, *Bernard Shaw* (London, 1961), pp. 255–6.

14. Huxley admitted this in the Introduction to the 1946 edition of *Brave New World*.
15. New York, 1923, p. 262.
16. "Three Books by Aldous Huxley," *The New Republic*, LXIX (February 10, 1932), 354.
17. London, 1960, p. 93.
18. *Encounter*, XIX (July 1962), 83.
19. New York, 1946, p. x.
20. *The Writer and the Absolute* (London, 1952), p. 154.
21. *Dickens, Dali and Others*, p. 121.
22. *The Road to Wigan Pier*, pp. 221–2.
23. Ibid. pp. 225–6.
24. Ibid. p. 233.
25. See Isaac Deutscher, *Heretics and Renegades and Other Essays* (London, 1955).
26. *Wigan Pier*, p. 234.
27. "True Pattern of H. G. Wells," *Manchester Evening News*, August 14, 1946, p. 1.
28. *Wigan Pier*, p. 234.
29. Ibid. p. 235.

CHAPTER VII

1. All are collected in C. S. Lewis, *Of Other Worlds. Essays and Stories*, ed. by Walter Hooper (London, 1966).
2. Quoted by Roger Lancelyn Green in *C. S. Lewis* (New York, 1963), p. 26.
3. Berkeley and Los Angeles, 1960.
4. *C. S. Lewis*, p. 26.
5. "Last Judgment" appeared in the first edition of *Possible Worlds* (London, 1927), and "Man's Destiny" in the second, American edition (New York, 1928).
6. *Into Other Worlds* (London and New York, 1958), p. 163.
7. "Man's Destiny," pp. 302–3.
8. *Modern Quarterly*, N. S. I (Autumn 1946), 32–40. Reprinted in Haldane, *Everything Has a History* (London, 1951).
9. "Man's Destiny," p. 304.

10. *Other Worlds,* pp. 76–7.
11. Letter to Wells dated October 16, 1931, now in the Wells Archive at the University of Illinois, Urbana.
12. See Wagar's discussion of Wells's impact on men like Haldane in *H. G. Wells and the World State,* p. 273.

CHAPTER VIII

1. *The Tale of the Future* (London, 1961); and *Checklist of Fantastic Literature* (Chicago, 1948).
2. See Donald Davidson, "The Shape of Things and Men: Two Views of the World State," *The American Review,* VII (1936), 225–48.
3. Occasionally, of course, there have been stories about the future, such as Hermann Hesse's *Magister Ludi* (1943), which stand outside the anti-utopian tradition and are unique in themselves. Although one literary historian has called Hesse's rich and complex novel "Wellsian," it is difficult to see how it is really so.
4. *The Times Literary Supplement,* May 20, 1960, p. 317.
5. *Inquiry into Science Fiction* (New York, 1955).
6. New York, 1953, pp. 108–9.
7. New York, 1953, p. 39.
8. Ibid. p. 83.
9. *New Maps of Hell,* p. 109.
10. London, 1955, p. 56.
11. New York, 1952, p. 260.

EPILOGUE

1. New York, 1965.
2. See Golding's two articles on science fiction, "Androids All," *Spectator,* CCVI (1961), 263; and "Astronaut by Gaslight," *Spectator,* CCVI (1961), 841–2.
3. In 1957 it was published in America as a Ballantine Science Fiction Classic, along with a novella by John Wyndham and another by Merwyn Peake.
4. "The World of William Golding," *Transactions and Proceedings of the Royal Society of Literature,* XXXII (1963), 44.
5. Quoted by Frank Kermode from a B.B.C. program in "The

Novels of William Golding," *International Literary Annual*, III (1961), 19.
6. Martin Green, "Distaste for the Contemporary," *The Nation*, CXC (May 21, 1960), 452.
7. A careful listing of Golding's other borrowing, not only from "The Grisly Folk" but also from *The Outline of History*, is given by Oldsey and Weintraub in *The Art of William Golding*, pp. 46–53.
8. *The Watchful Gods and Other Stories* (New York, 1950), pp. 179–80. The story was first published in *Yale Review*, XXI (September 1941), 53–60.
9. *A Sense of Reality* (London, 1963), p. 140.
10. New York, 1955, p. 144.
11. New York, 1963, p. 17.
12. Now reissued with a few additions, Frank Manuel (ed.), *Utopias and Utopian Thought*.
13. *Walden Two* (New York, 1960), p. 241.
14. Ibid. p. 243.
15. Ibid. p. 65.
16. Moura Budberg (trans.), *The Life and Thought of H. G. Wells* (London, 1966), p. viii. Kagarlitski's 15-volume edition of Wells's works, published in 1964, was printed in 350,000 copies.
17. Soviet science fiction has been published in America in three anthologies: Isaac Asimov (ed.), *Soviet Science Fiction* (New York, 1962); Asimov (ed.), *More Soviet Science Fiction* (New York, 1962); and Robert Magidoff (ed.) and Doris Johnson (trans.), *Russian Science Fiction* (New York, 1964). The collections edited by Asimov are reissues of two books distributed in this country by the Foreign Languages Publishing House, Moscow.
18. George Hanna (trans.), *Andromeda* (Moscow, n.d.), p. 205.
19. Ibid. p. 339.
20. *Daedalus*, XCIV (Spring 1965), 464.

SCIENCE FICTION AND UTOPIAN FANTASY

A Selected Bibliography of History
and Criticism

Allott, Kenneth. *Jules Verne*. London, 1940.

Amis, Kingsley. *New Maps of Hell*. New York, 1960.

Bailey, J. O. *Pilgrims Through Space and Time*. New York, 1947.

Bergonzi, Bernard. *The Early H. G. Wells*. Manchester, 1961.

Berneri, Marie Louise. *Journey Through Utopia*. London, 1950.

Bleiler, Everett. *Checklist of Fantastic Literature*. Chicago, 1948.

Bretnor, Reginald, ed. *Modern Science Fiction*. New York, 1953.

Butor, Michel. *Essais sur les modernes*. Paris, 1964.

Clarke, I. F. "The Nineteenth-Century Utopia," *Quarterly Review*, CCXCVI (1958), 80–91.

———. *The Tale of the Future . . . A Checklist*. London, 1961.

———. *Voices Prophesying War*. London, 1966.

Davenport, Basil. *Inquiry into Science Fiction*. New York, 1955.

De Camp, L. Sprague. *Science-Fiction Handbook*. New York, 1953.

Franklin, H. Bruce. *Future Perfect: American Science Fiction of the Nineteenth Century*. New York, 1966.

Gerber, Richard. *Utopian Fantasy*. London, 1955.

Green, Martin. *Science and the Shabby Curate of Poetry*. New York, 1965.

Green, Roger Lancelyn. *Into Other Worlds: Space Flight in Fiction, from Lucian to Lewis*. London and New York, 1958.

Hertzler, Joyce Oramel. *The History of Utopian Thought*. New York, 1923.

Hillegas, Mark R. "Dystopian Science Fiction: New Index to the Human Situation," *New Mexico Quarterly*, XXXI (1961), 238–49.

Kateb, George. *Utopia and Its Enemies*. New York, 1963.

Knight, Damon. *In Search of Wonder*. Chicago, 1956.

Kretzman, Edwin M. J. "German Technological Utopias of the Pre-War Period," *Annals of Science*, III (1938), 417–30.

Manuel, Frank, ed. *Utopias and Utopian Thought*. Boston, 1966.

Meyer, Karl E. *The New America: The Age of the Smooth Deal*. New York, 1961.

Morton, A. L. *The English Utopia*. London, 1952.

Moskowitz, Sam. *Explorers of the Infinite*. Cleveland, 1963.

———. *Seekers of Tomorrow*. Cleveland, 1966.

Mumford, Lewis. *The Story of Utopias*. New York, 1962.

Negley, Glenn, and J. Max Patrick. *The Quest for Utopia*. Garden City, 1962.

Nicolson, Marjorie Hope. *Voyages to the Moon*. New York, 1948.

Penzoldt, Peter. *The Supernatural in Fiction*. London, 1952.

Plank, Robert. "The Golem and the Robot," *Literature and Psychology*, XV (1965), 12–28.

Richards, D. J. "Four Utopias," *Slavonic and East European Review*, XL (1961), 220–28.

Russell, Frances Theresa. *Touring Utopia*. New York, 1932.

Schwonke, Martin. *Vom Staatsroman zur Science Fiction*. Stuttgart, 1957.

Walsh, Chad. *From Utopia to Nightmare*. New York and Evanston, 1962.

Woodcock, George. "Utopias in Negative," *Sewanee Review*, LXIV (1956), 81–97.

199

Wells, H. G. (*continued*)
  of the Worlds, 12, 17, 23–4,
  53, 55, 60, 145, 168; *When
  the Sleeper Wakes*, 4, 19, 25,
  31, 40, 41–9, 50, 57, 74, 93,
  94, 106, 107, 108, 111, 112,
  116, 124, 129, 130, 131, 132,
  161; *The Work, Wealth, and
  Happiness of Mankind*, 6;
  The World Set Free, 60, 62–
  3, 65, 103, 107, 109, 112, 153,
  168
Werfel, Franz, 148
West, Anthony, 17
West, Geoffrey, 17, 34, 64,
  182n, 183n
What Not, 145
Wiener, Norbert, 160

Wilbrandt, Konrad, 34
Williams, Charles, 138
Williamson, Jack, 155
"With Folded Hands," 155
Wolfe, Bernard, 186n
Woodcock, George, 83
Wyndham, John, 169, 171–2,
  188n

Yefremov, Ivan, 174, 175, 176–8

Zamyatin, Evgenii, 5, 147, 175;
  Herbert Wells, 101–4, 107,
  109, 130, 185n; *Litsa* [Faces],
  185n; "On Literature, Revolution, and Entropy," 104; "Tomorrow," 104; *We*, 3, 12, 20,
  34, 38, 82, 85, 97, 99–109,
  129, 133, 146, 150, 186n